Walking Through Paradise

Walking Through Paradise

Book Three in the Alpine Thru-Hiking series

Dan Colegate

Copyright © 2019 Dan Colegate

www.estheranddan.com

www.instagram.com/estheranddan

www.facebook.com/estheranddan

To Nana and Grandad, I hope you already know why x

Contents

Whatever Next

I can still remember exactly where I was when I first heard about the Vanoise National Park in the beautiful French Alps. I was a pale-faced undergraduate at the time, with a bum-fluff moustache and a hairline that was still good friends with my forehead. Partly I was pale because of a combination of ginger hair and British weather. However, even if it had been tropically sunny outside and I'd been blessed with a mane Brian May would've been proud of, it wouldn't have made much difference because, sadly, I spent most of my days in a darkened sub-basement surrounded by lasers and computer screens. In theory, I was trying to complete my chemistry degree by pushing back the boundaries of human understanding. In practice, I drank an unhealthy amount of sugary tea and played Queen music too loudly, staring into space and musing on what might become of my life.

On paper, I had a lot going for me. I was twenty-one years old and in just a few weeks' time I was going to have a first-class degree from Oxford University. I was in a relationship, albeit one I didn't fully understand, with a fellow student who seemed to accept my peculiarities. I was generally fit and healthy, a few long term issues notwithstanding. And despite all of the sugary tea (and biscuits) I still had all of my own teeth. And yet, despite these outwardly glowing prospects, the life I had worked so long to achieve suddenly seemed much less appealing to me.

The night before I heard about the Vanoise National Park I'd been to a careers event in a fancy hotel hosted by a multinational "consumer goods" company. In front of a room stuffed with several hundred eager young minds, a haggard and possibly hungover executive had declared that

1

"if you want a family, holidays and your weekends for yourself, we can accommodate that. But if you really want to succeed, we expect more."

The free food and 'all the cleaning products you can carry' had been the main reason I'd attended the event, a decision that seemed more than justified by the subsequent invention of liquitab baseball, but that foreboding message had still affected me. Was that really what I wanted? Had I agonised over GCSEs, A-levels, Oxbridge entry interviews and university finals to wear a crumpled suit and give my weekends over to faceless shareholders?

Probably, the answer was yes, I had. Without ever looking at it in quite those terms, that's precisely what I'd wanted as an ambitious teenager with above average grades and parents who I saw working so hard to look after me and my two younger brothers. Helping dad on his milkround had been awesome when I was ten years old, being allowed to get up at midnight to prepare the flask of tea and then roam the silent streets with a pint of silver-top in my little hands. But even then I knew that more was expected of me. *I* expected more of me. Specifically, based on school reports and such, it was a top class education that I was gunning for, an education that was bound to open whatever doors I chose to seek out. Doors that would lead to success, a big salary, a nice house and a shiny car. Probably even my own business cards. So yes, in hindsight, I had been aiming for the life of the crumpled suit and, one day, hopefully his boss's job as well.

Which is why, thanks to the help of an army of often silent supporters (who gave without expecting anything in return), I'd gotten myself into the situation that I had, knocking on the door of career success. In the arrogance of my youth I liked to think it was all down to me. 'My' hard work. 'My' talent. 'My' brains. In time I'd come to accept that wasn't the full story. Yes, I'd worked hard, but I'd also benefitted from passionate teachers, a loving family and a stable home, with parents and grandparents willing to go the extra mile to support me both at school and in my hobbies. We might not have been well-off financially, but those priceless gifts are ones that not everyone receives, regardless of their parents' bank balances.

Still, back in Oxford as a confused twenty-one year old who considered good grades and academic success as the main indicator of a life done properly, I was experiencing what may have been my very first existential crisis. What had it all been for? Did I really want what I'd worked for so long to achieve? What, when you got right down to it, was the point of life?

Perhaps that's why the moment that my good friend Tom, an older PhD student who I admired despite his love of jazz music, came into my darkened lair to tell me about his recent hiking trip sticks in my mind. Precisely what he told me about his tour around the Vanoise National Park, I no longer remember, but I do remember coming away with the overriding impression that it was like heaven on earth to look at. Evidently, I then passed that impression onto Esther when I got home as she remembers feeling exactly the same way.

The decade and a half after I finished my degree was eventful, unexpected and, more often than not, uncertain. Life unfolded erratically, as it so often does, the only constant being that somehow Esther and I remained together. Unsurprisingly, I didn't become a consumer goods chemist but instead sidestepped the career-decision bullet by hiding in academia for a while longer. I did a PhD and Esther completed a Master's degree at Durham University. We then both worked at Cambridge University while simultaneously trying to start our own online business, which we eventually left academia to work on full-time. Our primary goal was to create a life where we could spend more time together and maybe retire early one day. We also believed that our business idea could genuinely help people.

What came next is a story I've told before, in previous books, so here comes the short version. Life together, as business partners, was largely crap and we hated it.

A slightly longer version would say that although we were outwardly successful, winning awards and making a bit of money etc., behind closed doors we were unhappy, unhealthy and exhausted. Not only were we trying to create a big internet business and give the impression that we knew what we were doing to our investors and staff, but we also took on side projects like rental houses and private consultancy work. It wasn't long before our previously vibrant relationship became a hollow shell, bound together more by necessity and episodes of binge eating than by any romance. I had my own business cards, several different designs in fact depending on who I was meeting with, but with so many personas I wasn't sure who I even was any more.

It was ironic, I suppose, that in our attempt not to 'work for the man', we'd created the same sort of life that had so shaken me back in that Oxford hotel all those years earlier. The unshaven, crumpled suit, "if you really want to succeed, we expect more" type of life.

But, then again, wasn't this life of material success (and emotional scarcity) simply the natural extension of the life conditioning that had taken each of us to Oxford in the first place? I mean, our backgrounds may have been different in some ways, but in certain essentials they were a match. Both of us had challenging health conditions as children. Both of us were the first in our families to attend university. Both of us had been competitive athletes, Esther even rowing for Great Britain. Taking on extra work, projects and pursuits by 'pushing on' had always worked before. We could only hope it worked again this time, before we broke down, broke up, or both.

In many ways, the economic downturn of 2008 saved our physical and emotional health. Our business closed down, we sold much of the property, the consultancy work dried up and we both found ourselves in less demanding day jobs.

At first the change felt great, like sinking into a beloved armchair after a painfully bumpy journey, but it proved to be just a temporary relief. Something, during the previous few years of sleepless mornings connecting twenty hour working days, trapped in a relationship that had seen snuggling replaced by spreadsheets, seemed to have broken inside of us. We both had our own routes to diagnoses of depression, but the end result was the same. A listless sense of sadness with no apparent reason. We still had problems, of course, but then everyone has those. What was so infuriating was the feeling that our sense of dissatisfaction just didn't match our circumstances. At times I hated my life, but at others I hated myself for hating it.

So we tried making more changes. We took holidays again, the first since our student days. We planned date-nights. We focused on eating healthy meals and resuming regular exercise. But it was all tinkering around the edges. Each change bought a wave of optimism that always faded. Eventually, after a tumultuous year overshadowed by my having a series of unsuccessful surgeries linked to a lifelong, chronic condition, we decided to do something even more drastic. We decided to take a proper career break.

Yet even that we managed to overcomplicate. Instead of just buying a round-the-world plane ticket and sodding off, we decided we should get married first and also plan a six-month, two-thousand-kilometre hiking challenge along the GR5 trail that we'd call an 'extended honeymoon'. What can I say? It seemed like a good idea at the time, despite all of the stress and arguments that the seemingly endless arrangements threw into our lives.

Of course, the real reason we didn't feel able to just walk away and have fun was a combination of guilt and self-esteem issues. Everything we'd ever done had been a 'project' with a goal at the end, so we tried to make our career break into a project as well. I could say it was to stop other people judging us, which was partly true, but mostly it was our own judgements of ourselves that mattered. We simply needed an identity based on a difficult challenge. That way, if anyone asked what we were doing, we had an impressive answer. That we chose a long-distance hiking expedition as our challenge was due to a fairly recently discovered passion for tramping around the Lakeland fells, a seed that had been planted during a brief Easter getaway in our very first year together.

Unfortunately, or fortunately depending on how you look at it, life had other plans for us. It was just a few weeks before our wedding day and the beginning our long walk south that I found myself being cut open in an accident and emergency cubicle. A minor incisional hernia had appeared on my belly on Boxing Day, a relic of those unsuccessful surgeries I mentioned. With a February departure planned, we knew it needed fixing before I could trek with a heavy pack, which is why I felt so grateful to be offered a last-minute surgery slot on the NHS less than a month later. We never imagined I'd end up with a huge post-operative infection that would turn my abdomen into a deadly pus balloon.

Being the educated fool that I am, and a terrible patient, I ignored the fevers, the growing swelling and the increasing discolouration for almost a week until Esther insisted we get it looked at "just in case". A few hours later I heard the words "there's no time for anaesthetic", followed shortly afterwards by a lot of pain and an explosion of pus that hit the wall. You could say it was all downhill from there.

The surgeon who did what needed to be done to me later told Esther that in his opinion, with such a large abscess inside my body, I wouldn't have survived the night at home. More likely it would have burst internally, I would have slipped into toxic shock and died in my sleep. You could say that was the real wake-up call we'd been waiting for. Now all they had to do was knock me out properly so they could cut all of the infected tissue away and hope the necrotising fasciitis they suspected (also known as the flesh-eating disease) hadn't spread beyond the point of no return, because there's only so much 'middle' you can remove from a human body.

I woke up on a ward, my arms full of tubes and with a big chunk of my belly missing, but I was alive. Given the circumstances, I couldn't have hoped for better.

Three months after that, we drove away from Durham in "Homer", a second-hand motorhome that resembled a rolling mushroom on the outside and a 1970's living room on the inside. We'd had to cancel our wedding, as I'd been in hospital at the time, and during my long recovery we'd become officially unemployed thanks to the arrangements we'd already made. It was a strange limbo we'd fallen into, sat at home surrounded by half-made wedding decorations, reduced price Christmas cakes (that we'd planned to stack into a wedding cake) and shoeboxes full of home-made dehydrated meals that we were going to ask family to post out to us during our honeymoon hike.

Yet as soon as I received the all clear to travel, life seemed to conspire in our favour. It had taken just three weeks to sell our car, buy Homer, rent out our home, find new guardians for our house rabbits and put most of our worldly possessions into our mate Barry's attic. Everything flowed so effortlessly it almost felt like our original plans had been scuppered simply in order to set us down this new, even more exciting path.

When we did roll away from Durham for the first time in the spring of 2014 we told our friends and family that we'd be gone for a year. Secretly, we hoped it would be for longer, though neither of us ever imagined we'd still be going five years later.

What had started out as 'running away' had rapidly morphed into an odyssey of perspective-expanding adventures. Many of those adventures were physical ones, like hiking, cycling, rafting, diving, hot-air ballooning and trail-running, to name a few. All good things that we enjoyed very much. But the real life-changing adventures weren't the exclusively physical ones. They came from the people we met, the lifestyles we observed and the challenges of sharing a small motorhome full-time with a romantic partner. We saw new ways of carving out a life that we never would have imagined in a million years with our previously narrow perspective on what life was supposed to be about.

The internet abounds with slogans and memes about living like it's your last day, having no regrets and how love is the only true sign of a life well-lived, among other things. Yet until we travelled, that's all they were, slogans and memes. Nice to read for three seconds but not a viable approach to modern life. Travel, however, gave us a taste of something different. Not an ideal or a utopia, but just a sample of how it felt to let go of the future for a while and just exist. Frankly, after five years of nomadic life, we hardly even recognised ourselves as the two worrisome, goal-orientated, CV-focused, ten-year spreadsheet keeping control freaks who'd rattled south into the great unknown.

Sometimes, going with flow took us down some apparent dead-ends, but in hindsight even those dead-ends were really just adventures in disguise. None more so than the Spanish street dog we adopted who turned out to be pregnant. Just two weeks after Leela came to stay she gave birth to six more little dogs who we soon named George,

Bella, Rose, Pati, Jess and Teddy. Now that was a steep learning curve, but with the assistance of friends (and a lot of old newspapers) they grew into bundles of joy that lit up our lives.

A couple of months later, Jess and Teddy went to their new forever homes via friends of ours, and we couldn't have wished for better families for them to join. But, for one reason or another, the others stayed. As the subsequent weeks turned into months, we somehow built a life that contained five dogs and a motorhome. We all had to compromise a little, but there was no doubt that it was a love-filled, fur-tastic life we were sharing. It was busy and hard work and at times we were convinced that we were completely mad, but then we'd watch them all playing together in a field or lying all over of us on the bed, and we didn't want anything else. And besides, dog-hair is an under-rated condiment at meal times.

The one thing we couldn't do with so many dogs, however, was multi-day hiking trips. Which is how we get back to the Vanoise National Park and the still vivid memory of jazz-loving Tom's story. When Esther arranged for family and friends to look after different members of the pack for six or seven weeks in the summer of 2019, we knew the time had come to strap on our trail packs and take to the hills once more. We hadn't done any overnight trips since the summer before Leela came into our lives, a summer that had seen us set off from Geneva with an unopened guidebook, overfull rucksacks and a sense that we had some unfinished business to take care of regarding the GR5 trail. Our subsequent month in the mountains became my first travel book, *Turn Left At Mont Blanc*, which shares the full story of the ups, downs and many unexpected kindnesses we enjoyed on that marvellous adventure.

This time around, we decided to begin our summer of dog-free meanderings with an open-ended odyssey into the Swiss Alps. With no fixed plan or timescale in mind we went on to complete a giant loop around the Matterhorn, Europe's most iconic mountain, covering 320 kilometres in four weeks and climbing more than 25 vertical kilometres across some of Europe's finest passes (you can now read about the many peaks, glaciers and friendly faces we encountered in *Just Around The Matterhorn* if you like).

Yet when that adventure came to an end and we still had just over three weeks left until we had to pick up the fluffier members of our gang, we weren't quite ready to stop. Well, actually, that's not strictly true. I was fairly ready to stop because I'd been seriously ill during part of our Matterhorn tour. It was some sort of virus that had laid me low after two and a bit weeks of hiking, forcing me into a hotel bed where I'd sweated and shivered in equal measure for forty eight hours before finally being able to get back on my feet. Unfortunately, even then, my troubles weren't over as my mouth had filled up with ulcers that made it incredibly painful for me to eat. We'd gotten through it, somehow, and I was almost back to normal by the end of the four weeks. Even so, I have to admit that I'd initially not wanted to go multi-day hiking again straight away.

"Let's just stay in the motorhome and do some day hiking" I'd suggested.

But Esther has a voracious appetite for the great outdoors and it was going to be her birthday in mid-September, so in the end the old romantic in me offered it up as a sort of gift. I even promised not to grumble if it rained a lot (although I had my fingers crossed when I said it).

"Just two weeks though, and we take it easy" I insisted, getting a big hug as an answer. Of course, I knew I'd enjoy it just as much as Esther once we were back out there and lost in the hills again. I just have a weakness for fluffy pillows that makes the first few steps away from urban comforts a bit of a wrench. As soon as I get far enough away, the cord is cut and I can't imagine anything other than mountain life.

Anyway, agreeing upon two more weeks gave us the beginnings of a plan. The only question now was where should we spend those two weeks?

I think you already know the answer.

Getting There

Of course, Tom wasn't the only person who had ever mentioned the Vanoise National Park to us over the years. Many other hikers we'd met from all corners of the world had name-dropped the Vanoise as a personal highlight of theirs, including during our just completed Matterhorn tour.

During our motorhome adventures we'd visited the French Alps more than once, usually to cycle up the various long, steep and winding roads made famous as part of the Tour de France. During those visits we'd often looked at the irregular outline of the Vanoise on the map and taken a moment to reflect on what treasures lay within those weaving boundaries? Yet for some reason, we'd never felt it was quite the right time, or the best weather, or the location to explore it from.

The closest we'd got was when we'd cycled up and over the 2764 metre Col de l'Iseran, the highest paved road pass in the Alps, which just tickles the easternmost boundary of the park. But we did that one October as part of the Route des Grande Alpes, a 700 kilometre cycling route between Nice and Geneva, and it was so bitingly cold and windy that any thought of exploring on foot was pushed firmly to the back of our minds as we hurriedly drove our motorhome towards the next road pass on our list. But we knew it was there, waiting for us to explore it one day. Now, it seemed, that day had arrived.

The Vanoise National Park was formally established in 1963, the first of ten National Parks to be created in France (seven on the mainland and three in its overseas departments). With its northernmost boundary less than 10 miles south of Mont Blanc, its irregular shape defies any sort of simple description. For a while I thought that a distorted triangle might make sense, but frankly it doesn't do justice to the meandering line of a park boundary shaped by valleys, peaks, glaciers, ski-slopes and, for one fourteen kilometre section, the national border with Italy. It's a very special section of border, however, because on the other side of it lies the Italian Gran Paradiso National Park which was formally twinned with the Vanoise in 1972 to create a nature reserve of over 1250 square kilometre (just under 500 square miles). That makes it the largest nature reserve in Western Europe.

No outside exploitation whatsoever is permitted within the Vanoise National Park boundary, and while a limited amount of traditional livestock grazing is allowed in summer, there is no permanent habitation inside the Vanoise either. As a result, the area abounds with wildlife, especially ibex and marmot who are common sights on the slopes of the hundred or so 3000 metre summits in the park (the tallest being La Grande Casse at 3855 metres). No wonder it's described by so many people as a green jewel in the Alpine range, a place of unspoiled beauty and natural harmony.

Accordingly, rules for visitors to the Vanoise National Park are strict and simple, most of them being rules you should always observe in the wilderness, including no littering, no picking of flowers, no straying from footpaths (to limit erosion) and no unnecessary noise to disturb animals. But then the park rules go a little further. Mountain biking is also not allowed in the park, or dogs (even on a lead) and nor is wild camping permitted anywhere within the park boundaries. In most of France a distinction is made between camping, with deck chairs and barbeques for example, as opposed to bivouacking, where a one-night, small-tent pitch is allowed provided it's discrete and out of sight of other dwellings. But in the Vanoise, even bivouacking is strictly forbidden, except directly outside of certain refuges.

Having just finished a four week tour that involved a fair amount of blissfully remote, high-altitude bivouacking, this would be a big change for us but one we intended to respect completely, without question. In other parts of the Alps wild camping rules are sometimes a grey area, and we'd often asked farmers, hotel owners or local tourist offices for guidance on where we might pitch a tent for a single night, arriving late, leaving early and leaving no trace of our presence. But in the Vanoise there is no grey area. And since we respect and applaud the national park system, we had no intention of trying to break any rules within its boundaries.

Then again, by relying on the many refuges in and around the park, we expected we'd have no reason to. Our four weeks in the Swiss and Italian Alps may have been an ad-hoc, DIY route that we made up as we went along, but this time we intended to stick to a much more conventional plan (probably).

Our chosen guidebook was the popular "Tour Of The Vanoise: A Trekking Circuit Of The Vanoise National Park" by Kev Reynolds (Cicerone Guides). Within its pages was a proposed eleven-day circuit of the park, tracing out a wonky bow-tie shape that almost met itself in the middle, in addition to a series of shorter loops, detours and alternative stages for those with less time in hand. The main route amounted to a 154 kilometre trek, mostly hugging the park boundary, with over 7000 metres of ascent along the way. That sounded okay to us. It was September after all, the days were getting shorter and having just completed a 320 kilometre walk (including 25,000 metres of climbing), this sounded perfect. It would be beautiful, sensible and we'd still have some time in hand to pursue any detours that sprang to mind. During our Matterhorn tour we'd even come up with a name for especially spectacular and challenging little add-ons, "Esther's magical mystery detours", a nod towards their usual mastermind.

The five days we'd given ourselves between our two tours flew by in a blur of eating, sleeping and titbits of simple preparation, such as trying to find a decent map of the Vanoise National Park. Perhaps unsurprisingly, after four weeks largely in the vast remoteness of the mountains, our resilience to busy roads and hot superstores had dwindled somewhat. As a result, although we were enjoying the physical recuperation time we'd earmarked for ourselves, mentally we felt a little lost when we descended back into the hustle and bustle. Exhaust fumes, traffic jams, litter piles blown into corners and incessantly moving people everywhere we looked. It was like an alien world at first, a chance to look at the urban sprawl with fresh eyes and wonder if it really needed to be like this? It was the same way we always felt after a sojourn in the wilderness, so we sort of expected it, but it was still a huge relief when the time came to get into position for our next adventure.

Our chosen starting point was the village of Pralognan-la-Vanoise, on the north-west corner of the park at 1418 metres altitude. In terms of the guidebook itinerary this was actually the end of stage 9, but it was a loop so it didn't really matter where we started. The guidebook actually suggested starting in Modane, a larger town with better transport links for people arriving by plane and train on the other side of the park. But we didn't need any of that, quite the opposite in fact. Mostly what we wanted was a quiet place to park our motorhome for the fortnight we expected to be away, something the Pralognan tourist office assured us we could find with them.

We left the valley floor at Moûtiers, initially following signs for the well-known ski resorts of Meribel and Courchevel. It was only at this point I remembered that I must have been this way once before, sixteen years earlier, during a student ice hockey tour of the French Alps. We'd toured for ten days way back in January 2003, winning in front of packed ice rinks full of English-speaking ski-tourists mostly cheering for the Oxford Blues (because they had nothing better to do). Yet it was only when I saw the names of the places we'd played on the road signs that I realised I had almost no recollection of any of it. Just random flashbacks.

Then again, I did once see a photograph of me sleeping with a fully decorated eight-foot Christmas tree on that tour, so perhaps I shouldn't be surprised to have such hazy memories. I also remember a fan asking me to autograph her cleavage, the first and only time that will ever happen to me. Turns out it's surprisingly difficult to write on a soft, bouncy surface with a felt tip pen! Honestly, rock stars have a tough time of it, and I speak as one who's lived their life for a whole eight seconds, or maybe even ten.

Lost in such nostalgic reflections, I ignored the subsequent turnings up to those ski resorts and continued right to the end of the road at Pralognan, where we were relieved to find exactly what the tourist office staff had described to us on the phone. It was a quiet car park, not totally deserted and just a stone's throw from the main thoroughfare. Just what we hoped for.

Now that we were here, in theory, we had very little left to do in order to be ready to start hiking again the next morning. We'd already bought trail food down in the valley and since it had only been four days since we'd finished our four-week Matterhorn tour, most of our camping and hiking gear was still packed. We'd washed our dirt-encrusted hiking clothes in an actual washing machine (as opposed to a mountain stream or bathroom sink), and had also aired out our waterproofs, tent and sleeping bags etc. during one especially sunny afternoon, but apart from that we hadn't changed anything else. It was, essentially, ready to go, and at just 10 kilograms for me and 7 kilograms for Esther (excluding food and water), we felt we'd already done pretty well in the packing department. We'd definitely come a long way from the couple who used to haul twenty five kilogram packs into the Lake District for a single night of wild camping a decade earlier.

Some of the changes had been down to investing in good kit, while the rest had come from learning to trust that kit and not pile on extra kilograms with countless 'just in case' spares. I honestly can't tell you how many spare pairs of socks and fleeces I used to cram into every nook and cranny of my 85-litre rucksack! It all added up. Plus, it was often a false economy financially as well as leading to unpleasant bruises and chafing. As the saying goes, "if you buy cheap, you buy twice" and hiking equipment was an area where that had certainly proved true for us.

When we first started hiking regularly, I used to go through a 'waterproof' coat every year. I bought them from budget outlet stores and every time I was disappointed to find that 'waterproof' actually just meant that the water soaked through slowly. As a consequence, rainy day walks had always been a matter of counting the minutes until my underpants got soaked. But since we'd used eBay to get some great deals on some slightly more expensive Gore-Tex coats from premium hiking brands, we'd been using the same ones for years and they showed no signs of wearing out.

Another example was our rucksacks. After years of sweaty, uncomfortable and heavy ex-military stuff, we'd gone for packs from the Osprey Exos product line that weighed just 1.1 kilograms each, saving a whole kilogram on most other packs of similar size. We also each had Rab Infinity 300 down sleeping bags, which weighed just 650 grams but were still graded down to a 0°C comfort temperature. Our air mattresses were Thermarest NeoAir (300 grams), our saucepan and gas burner were made of titanium, our Black Diamond headtorches could shine like car headlights when required, our Leki hiking poles were carbon fibre and our Rab down jackets were part of an Everest base camp recommended kit list once upon a time.

Not everything we used was top quality, but the stuff that was had mostly been found on eBay and was still going strong after at least five or six years of frequent use. A bit frayed at the edges perhaps, but functional nonetheless.

Like most things in life, pack weight on the trail exists on a spectrum. Pack a lot of stuff and you can be more comfortable and cleaner in the evenings, perhaps with multiple changes of clothes and even floral-scented shower gel, but you have to carry it all day, which can hurt. Pack very little stuff and you can walk further every day with less effort, but you have to learn to do without as many creature comforts when you stop, when you sleep or when the weather gets bad.

Be careful though, for those who start down the rabbit hole of weight saving can often become obsessive, marvelling at the latest gadgets and featherlight devices like a toddler with a toffee apple. 'Ultralighting', as it's called, is a popular movement in the hiking world, with people vying to cut their pack weights down ever further using a combination of cutting-edge material technology and ingenious DIY solutions. Or just snapping their toothbrush handles in half and cutting labels out of their coats.

Probably we fell somewhere in the middle. We had snapped our toothbrush in half and Esther had cut the labels out of various things (much to my annoyance at the time), but although we were happy to forego toiletries, spare clothes and unnecessary 'backups' nowadays, we weren't yet ready to replace our full length air mattresses with a silver foil blanket on a bed of leaves, or our decently spacious tent with a tarp attached to our trekking poles. Which is why we were still some way off ultralight nirvana, but considering that our packs had a sturdy frame, comfortable hip straps and contained cooking gear, a two-person tent, warm and comfortable sleeping equipment, head torches, base layers to sleep in, just two spare pairs of socks each and one pair of pants, waterproofs, a camera, phones and chargers, plus a few other things like the medical equipment I needed to use each day, we thought we'd done fairly well.

Then again, you can always improve and things do wear out eventually, so with half a day in hand now that we'd arrived in Pralognan, we decided to take a browse around town to see if there was any bargain kit that caught our eye. Esther's boots, for example, were knackered and she could do with some new footwear. My own had fallen apart (literally) during our Matterhorn tour and I'd had to buy some new chunky ones on-the-fly in Zermatt. Esther's weren't far off going the same way and although she really wanted the same type again, we weren't sure we could wait another fortnight in order to get her the specific model online.

We also had half an eye on upgrading our headtorches which, although 'storm-proof', were heavy and got so little use it seemed an unnecessary 400 gram burden. Then there were our hiking poles to consider. One of Esther's had already snapped on the Matterhorn tour, replaced by a donated and slightly bent aluminium one, while the 'expander-lock' mechanisms on the remaining three were starting to fail from time to time. We could make do for another fortnight, probably, but if there was a good offer on a more modern, lightweight alternative, we'd seriously consider it.

Two hours later we both had new shoes, new headtorches and new trekking poles! Pralognan, it turned out, had very little open at this time of year, but what was open were almost all hiking equipment stores. One in particular had a fantastic sale on much of the previous season's items and, because they were closing at the weekend until winter season, were willing to offer us further reductions on a bundle purchase. As a result, we'd somehow stumbled across exactly what we were looking for at better than half price.

The shoes we'd both opted for were a bit of a gamble, but at just 80 euros a pair (down from 175 euros recommended retail price because they were last year's colours) we'd decided to take the risk. We'd talked a few times about hiking in lightweight walking shoes instead of boots, foregoing a little ankle support in favour of less weight and more agility, so when we stumbled across the last two pairs of Salomon XA Pro 3D GTX, the same brand as our much-loved hiking boots and in our sizes, we decided it was time to finally try.

The other new items were a pair of Petzl Bindi headtorches (just 34 grams each!) and Black Diamond Carbon Z trekking poles (284 grams a pair). That meant a total weight saving of more than 600 grams but, even more importantly, replacing some worn out poles and unnecessarily bomb-proof head-torches with something more suited to our needs. We'd make sure the old bits had a new life with other people down the line, but for now we went back to the motorhome and, enthused by our shiny lightweight gear, put everything else in our packs back under the microscope.

How many paracetamol do we need? How many silver safety blankets? Why did we take two spare pairs of socks around the Matterhorn? And two pack towels? How much does this chunky compass weigh compared to this tiny one in that whistle? Why do we have a charger for each phone and the camera when they all have the same size adapter? Can you remember ever actually using these mosquito headnets? Why did we take aluminium bottles *and* water bladders? Isn't there a spare water bladder in the cupboard instead? And so the assessment continued.

By the time darkness had fallen we'd somehow managed to rid our packs of an estimated three kilograms of 'stuff' compared to our Matterhorn tour (including the savings from our new gear). Sure, we no longer had a serious first aid kit, we'd be more vulnerable to mosquito swarms, we couldn't charge a camera *and* a phone at the same time and we'd be sharing a single sawn-off toothbrush again (we'd done it before), but it all felt very satisfying. We'd even gone so far as to detach the seven-centimetre tall, twenty-gram cuddly giraffe we called Gerald from my pack, despite him having joined us on every other hike we'd done (needless to say, he wasn't best pleased).

We thought we'd been minimalist around the Matterhorn, but now, with the equipment we currently owned at least, our packs were truly stripped down to the absolute bare bones for survival in the wild. With food and water thrown in, Esther was perhaps carrying 9 kilograms and myself around 14 kilograms. Not too shabby. All we had to do now was try and overcome our excitement in order to get some sleep.

Roll on the adventure!

Three In One

We began our tour of the Vanoise National Park on a fine September morning. Our clothes smelled like lavender, our packs were dry and our shoes were out-of-the-box new, but although we were just a few metres away from our motorhome and still shockingly clean, we'd now left that world behind and had entered into the unknown. It was time to cut the cord of comfort.

Ahead of us lay countless new sights and spectacles, challenges and rewards, people to meet and unfamiliar places to rest our head. We didn't know how the next fortnight would unfold, but we did know that whatever we encountered would be a unique and unrepeatable sequence of events. The people we'd cross paths with, the marmots who'd emerge, the ibex who would look down on us, even the flowers that would flutter in the wind. None of it would ever be quite the same ever again. Nobody, not even us, would ever be able to fully reproduce the experience we were about to enjoy, which I think is a pretty awesome way of looking at life.

As fate would have it, the parking we were using was directly next to a small graveyard and our motorhome was positioned right against the edge of it. Our door opened directly onto a view of headstones and decorative script recording the names and dates of lives that had now ended. Who knew what adventures they'd enjoyed, or perhaps not had the opportunity to take?

"What adventures do you think we'll have today?" we said in unison, each of us feeling the gravity and the symbolism of our opening view as we leaned in to attempt the clumsy embrace required to reach behind each other's rucksacks. It was a mantra we'd taken to saying during our Matterhorn tour and which was our little way of taking a second to remember how fortunate we were. Fortunate to be alive. Fortunate to be in the mountains. And fortunate to have enough health and fitness in this moment to go and explore them.

We strode quickly along Pralognan's high street in search of the trail markers that would point us towards the park boundary and the wilderness beyond. Because of the way the park is defined, with only undeveloped tundra inside and (almost) all roads and human constructions outside, its boundary is an erratic line that weaves about like a drunken spider. We'd woken up just 500 metres from the park and would remain so for the next eight or nine kilometres of hiking before we actually crossed the boundary ourselves. That meant there would be plenty to see before we got there, but there was still something alluring about the dark green line on our map that made us eager to get across and formally enter the protected spaces beyond.

Our guidebook told us that the suggested stage from Pralognan (Stage 10) was a four hour, twelve kilometre trek up to the Refuge de Pèclet-Polset at 2474 metres altitude. Apparently, despite the thousand metres of altitude gain, this would be "undemanding". Because we were getting going in mid-morning we were well aware that we could choose to continue further if we wanted to, provided we got to another permitted bivouacking refuge or left the park again before pitching our tent. But that was a decision we'd have to make later in the day. A four hour stage was shorter time-wise than many of our recent days hiking around the Matterhorn but a thousand metres of climbing is hard work, whichever way you approach it. We specifically wanted to take it easier on this adventure by following the itinerary, or at least that was what we'd told ourselves.

That said, as we set out in the morning sunshine where we ended up by nightfall didn't really feel like it mattered very much. It would no doubt seem important when the time came, but that time was still a whole day of

23

blue skies and footsteps away. Until then we just wanted to put one foot in front of the other and explore the green wilderness we could see unfolding away from us.

Despite our excitement at stripping down our packs the night before, they were still reassuringly hefty on our backs now that they were fully laden with bulging water bladders and about four days' worth of food. But it was a reassuring rather than an oppressive weight, solid instead of painful. Partly this was because we were in decent shape after our previous adventure but it was also psychological. There was a physical comfort that came from knowing we'd packed sensibly and had nothing unnecessary or thoughtless weighing us down. I still remember effing and blinding at each other three days into our first big thru-hiking trip towards Mont Blanc, each of us throwing blame at each other for trying to walk too high and too far with too much 'effing' weight on our backs. It had been a steep learning curve, in more ways than one.

This time, however, we had the reassurance that we were humping only the barest of our personal version of 'essentials' on our backs. I still had a slight nagging sense of unease in the pit of my stomach, but that was just my comfort-seeking demons still grumbling about leaving our lovely soft motorhome bed behind. I knew they'd go away by the time we got the tent set up. Or, even if they didn't, it would be too late for them to moan anyway. Sometimes I really feel like there are two Dans occupying my body, a loner who thinks a three-word sentence is uncomfortable and would be quite happy in a cave with a stack of books, and a garrulous adventure lover who wants to dance up mountains and bathe in waterfalls. Most of the time they get along fairly well, but sometimes the tension gets a bit too much and I end up having an argument with myself, which makes me grumpy. Not this time though. Bookish Dan was just going to have to take one for the team. Besides, I'd already promised him he could read all through October and didn't even have to go jogging if he didn't want to.

We left town on the winding main road, clicking along the tarmac with our pristine featherlight poles before entering into a forested section of gently rising trails. Our first destination was the hamlet of Les Prioux, which we passed after only three quarters of an hour, just as the trees thinned to reveal a wide, green and flat-bottomed valley stretching away south until the green shaded into grey and the ground climbed towards the sky.

We continued through Les Prioux, still following the road until the tarmac turned into gravelly dirt at a small car park. This was the end of the road, literally. On the surrounding fields families and elderly couples were laying out picnic blankets and preparing for lunch beneath the now hot sun. The sky above us was brilliant blue without a single trace of cloud anywhere to be found. It may have been September but the mood was still very much the height of summer. Not too busy though, which it perhaps had been back in mid-August. There were only a couple of dozen people milling around and a similar amount strung out along the open hillside trail we could see.

We'd only been walking for an hour and half so decided not to stop for lunch ourselves, crossing the bubbling river and beginning a slightly more serious climb up the western side of the valley. The track was wide and the gradient, as promised, remained undemanding for almost the entire time. A few short rises reminded our thighs that they were back on the job, but even with the mellow slope the heat of the sun still had us sweating strongly into our fresh-smelling hiking clothes.

As we climbed the distant sight of the long Glacier de Gébroulez drifted into view on our right, glinting as it flowed down the northern slopes of the Aiguille de Polset. And that's when we crossed the park boundary. It was just a little sign, a bland yellow and green noticeboard reinforcing the rules of the park, but it felt like a special moment for us and we found ourselves feeling renewed excitement. We'd arrived. We were in the Vanoise!

Because the climb had been so gentle for so long our height gain and the associated changes in scenery had been almost imperceptible, until now. It was almost a shock to look up and find that those grey-tinted slopes that had looked so distant from Les Prioux had moved very much closer and had formed into towering cliffs. Behind us was no longer a road surrounded by occasional buildings but a pale, softly-curved valley with nothing but a small stream and a nearby off-white dirt track to suggest any human influence at all. Yet still we climbed higher, inching ever closer to the visually sharp boundary which separated the world of green pastures from the panorama of grey and white rock that was now hanging above us.

By the time our nominal destination, the Refuge de Pèclet-Polset, drew into sight away on our right, we were stood in the shadow of glaciers and peaks that had been nothing but a distant imagining that morning. Our map provided names of various features, but it was the overall effect we wanted to bask in. The overriding sense of spaciousness and freedom that comes from standing like an ant beneath jagged ridgelines and tooth-like crags which burst out of the chaos of scree that characterises the transition between hillside and mountainside.

Taking stock of our situation, it was mid-afternoon and we had indeed taken the suggested four hours of hiking time to reach this point. We hadn't been rushing but we hadn't exactly been ambling either, so it seemed the guidebook timings were a fair estimate of our pace for the time being. Had we been anywhere else in the Alps, and bivouacking in the wild permitted, we would have continued on without a second thought. Mid-afternoon felt far too soon to stop for the day, especially when the weather was so warm and fine.

But this wasn't anywhere in the Alps, it was the Vanoise. We either camped outside of the Refuge de Pèclet-Polset or we had to commit to at least another three to four hours of hiking, which was how long we reckoned it would take us to reach the park's southern boundary via a crossing of the 2796 metre Col de Chavière (the highest crossing on the tour).

From there, we could either continue all the way down into Modane, an 1800 metre descent, or take an alternative route downhill and cut the corner on Modane completely. That would save us almost 1000 metres of down-and-up and leave us squarely back on the guidebook itinerary at the Refuge de l'Orgère, the next place we'd be permitted to bivouac at 1935 metres. Granted, we'd have skipped the whole of 'Stage 1' out of Modane, but as far as we could see Modane was mostly in the guidebook as a convenient starting point rather than an especially pleasant feature.

Choosing to dodge the down-and-up into Modane was a no-brainer. Quite why we chose to push on and do seven hours of hiking on our very first day, I'm less certain. It was exactly the opposite of the approach we'd resolved to take, especially when there was a pleasant, sun-dappled refuge just a stone's throw away from us, with oodles of baking green hillside just begging to be dozed upon. But we chose to keep walking. In hindsight, I can see it's just how we got our kicks. We just loved the walking part of our adventures, the forward motion, the excitement at getting to the next viewpoint and peering around the next bend in the trail. The lounging around at the end of the day part has never been as exciting to us.

The trail became even quieter once we'd passed the Refuge de Pèclet-Polset, winding upwards through a still moderate series of rises and falls while the ground beneath our feet slowly transitioned from grass to stone. The teeth of the high ridgeline to our left seemed to grow as we drew closer and it wasn't long until we could clearly distinguish the black saddle of the Col de Chavière on the southern horizon.

With about a hundred and fifty metres still to climb we rounded a large mound of dirt and gravel to discover that we'd entered into a garden of cairns. Thousands upon thousands of stone piles stretched away from us on the otherwise bare plateau, constructed in all shapes, sizes and levels of intricacy that stood out starkly against the grey cliffs beyond. It was a beautiful and beguiling sight in such an otherwise desolate landscape. Most cairns were small and simple but some constructions were engineering marvels, appearing to defy gravity as monolithic slabs were suspended on fragile stilts and teetering towers of tiny pebbles.

Pausing only briefly to create our own three-stone masterpiece, we began weaving carefully through the sculptures (for that is what they were), continuing to creep closer to the saddle and the remaining scree slopes that would carry us towards it. A few dirty snow patches were still defying the hot summer sun, their pock-marked surfaces resembling an off-white moonscape in miniature, but whether they would manage to see the next winter or not was still uncertain even though it was September. Probably they wouldn't last if this late season heat continued much longer.

Although there are many higher crossings in the Alps, the 2796 metre Col de Chavière is the highest on any of the major GR trails that span Europe and so demands appropriate respect. To hike across broken chunks of mountain so close to 3000 metres is an experience that requires a calm head and confident feet and even despite our Matterhorn tour occasionally taking us much higher still (above 3600 metres at times), it was not something we had grown de-sensitised to. A few hours earlier we had been in our motorhome, surrounded by tarmac and bricks. Now all we could see was snow, ice and rock, with a final steep ascent up a shifting slope that was entirely in keeping with such a lofty crossing.

The view from the stony col when we reached it was like a border between two worlds. Behind us, mostly what we could see were pale grey or dark peaks topped with snow, with just a few patches of green valley still visible between us and the unmistakable shape of Mont Blanc on the distant northern horizon. Ahead of us, the saddle fell away sharply into rough ground, with a scree slope sweeping in from the right and the fragile thread of the trail weaving through the uneven terrain towards a green hanging valley far below. In the centre of the scene was the triangular mini-peak of the Tête Noire, dividing the lip of the hanging valley in two, while beyond that the southern horizon was a jumble of intricate hills rolling towards the distant Ecrins National Park and the Barre des Ecrins, Europe's most southerly 4000 metre summit that rose above it all.

We couldn't linger too long since we had designs on reaching the Refuge de l'Orgère before twilight arrived. The descent from the col was steep and loose at first but soon eased into firmer ground, with an obvious trail tracking through the hanging valley. In what seemed like no time at all we had gone from a stone shoulder in a land of summits to a sea of green looking back up at bare ridges and cliffs. We aren't geologists, so had no idea what we were looking at in terms of names, but the sheer number of colours and rock formations we could see around us was dazzling.

The trail crossed the hanging valley and then split, the main tour route (the GR55) branching to the right of the Tête Noire and our variant branching left. A steep, zig-zag descent followed, a knee-straining effort which took us down a forested hillside and back out of the Vanoise National Park.

That we had passed all the way through a section of the park in just a few hours is an indication of how the irregular shape of the boundary encloses countless lumps and bumps of geography. We were just a kilometre or so from re-entering the park, if we chose, but now that we were outside of it we could technically pitch our tent again even though the Refuge de l'Orgere was still a little way off.

It was getting dusky in the sky when we did reach the refuge, a chunky grey stone building at the end of narrow access road running up from the main valley far below. We could have gone straight inside and asked about bivouacking but something held us back. Perhaps it was because after such a peaceful day we wanted to stay a little anonymous. Or maybe it was because we'd grown so used to wild camping during our previous tours. Either way, we made a snap decision not to go inside after all and instead find a nearby spot to pitch our tent discreetly.

Turning north, we made our way along a flat, gravel-constructed walking trail in search of a good spot that was out of sight of the various other dwellings we could see around us. There were perhaps a dozen or so picturesque summer lodges strung out along the narrow inlet of 'non-park' ground we were in, most of them already locked down for winter from what we could see. The valley was only a few hundred metres across at this point, with steeply rising walls that raced up towards the park boundary on both sides, leaving just this finger of idyllic holiday cottages in between.

Just a few minutes along the trail we encountered a small herd of donkeys, which we always love because they tend to be so inquisitive and friendly. One fellow in particular seemed especially excited to see us, trotting straight over and nuzzling his grey snout into our chests in search of fuss. It worked. 'Dusty' got a good ten minutes of our attention after that, the name coming from the fact he was literally very dusty, with each pat sending a cloud into the air and leaving us with our own thin coating. By the time we walked on, it seemed we'd gained a companion as Dusty began trotting determinedly behind us. A small part of me was worried we were stealing someone's donkey, but mostly I quite liked the fact he was following us. Esther and I love all animals, so if a 200 kilogram bloke who didn't talk too much wanted to join our team, I was okay with that. Sadly, he only followed us for a few hundred metres.

We ended up pitching our tent right in the sharp v-shaped tip of the valley. We'd walked about a kilometre from the refuge and were still on the path, but we couldn't go any further without climbing back towards the park boundary. Since we were out of sight of any buildings and had a water source nearby, we reasoned this was a good enough spot. Besides, it was past seven o'clock by now and we were coming down from the excitement of the day, our tired limbs and empty bellies firmly letting us know we needed a sit down and some food. We might have intended to take it easy on this tour but had, in a way, just completed three guidebook stages in one (if you ignore the fact we'd cut the corner on Modane and saved a lot of climbing). Either way, stages 10, 11 and 1 were now behind us.

Our secluded little valley head had lost the sun some time ago and the temperature was falling quickly, but a portion of scalding lentil pasta with tomato puree and a little stem ginger sliced into it soon warmed us up from the inside. With a fantastic purple sky framed by the shape of the valley's sides, we hunkered down outside of our tent to bask once again in the magical simplicity of tent life in the high mountains. Not an easy life, far from it, but we had no internet, phone signal, television or even artificial lighting to disturb and stimulate us. All we could was sit back in silence and appreciate the sliver of crescent moon hanging in the sky above us. Which is precisely what we did, holding each other tightly and leaning back against a handy tuft of slightly damp grass. Not a bad first day at all really.

Vital Statistics – Day 1
Start: Pralognan-la-Vanoise
End: Close to Refuge de l'Orgere
Distance Hiked: 22 kilometres
Hiking Time: 7 hours
Height Gain: 1380 metres
Height Loss: 860 metres

People

It was a cold dawn with a sheen of frost on the ground to indicate that, despite the hot sunshine of the previous day, the season was changing slowly around us. We ate a bit of fruit in our tent before packing up quickly in the growing light and then happily discovering a host of delicious wild raspberries on the trail back towards the Refuge de l'Orgere.

We had briefly considered adapting the guidebook itinerary once more, this time by climbing straight from our overnight spot towards the 2923 metre Col de la Masse. We'd have ultimately gone in the same direction as the guidebook route but via a much higher altitude 'shortcut', at least as the crow flies anyway. However, the clouds we could see gathering quickly above the col had made our minds up for us, which is why we were tramping back towards the refuge to pick up the main route again.

Sadly, Dusty wasn't waiting on the path to greet us, although some of his less forward friends were watching us from a distance, and we regained the main tour trail after just quarter of an hour of plodding. From the outside the refuge looked deserted, but the steady stream of people we could see walking away from it and the young couple packing up their tent in the trees outside suggested otherwise. Oftentimes we take a peek inside of refuges to appreciate their uniqueness, since no two are ever quite the same, but since we'd only just got moving and it was still chilly we decided to press on this time.

We navigated the short descent from the refuge onto grassy meadows and then began a long traverse of the park boundary heading east. Mostly encased in pine forest, the route climbed gradually via a series of dusty, stony paths that occasionally zig-zagged uphill a little more steeply. Hanging high above the Maurienne valley below, occasional views down into the sprawling industrial-looking mass of Modane were tempered by far-reaching views east towards silhouettes of mountains looming out of the haze. Visibility wasn't great, especially when one of the many fast-moving clouds drifted over the sun, but the sense of being a little hidden from the rest of the world created a private atmosphere, almost as though this was our own hillside for a while. Although we knew there were people striding ahead of us, we were yet to actually see anyone close up and, because we kept stopping to pick more wild raspberries and even a few strawberries, we were unlikely to catch anybody up soon.

After a time the path carried us out onto a more open shoulder of rock, tracing over the contours of the mountainside and still slowly gaining height until we reached the broad expanse of the Col du Barbier at 2287 metres. Although we'd 'only' gained three hundred metres overall, it had felt like more due to the long traverse that had taken us a couple of hours already.

In a sense the Col du Barbier isn't really a true col at all, because the southern side only rises a tiny amount before falling away into the valley. The overall effect is of a saddle with a section missing. It does command magnificent views of the surrounding area though. To the east, the direction we were going in, the hulking grey mass of La Dent Parrachee dominates the sky line above two large reservoirs, while to the south the wide sweep of the Maurienne valley cuts through the landscape. From our vantage point we could even see a cluster of small buildings on the hillside beneath La Dent Parrachee which we assumed (correctly as it turned out) to be our destination for the day, the Refuge de Plan Sec.

It wasn't even midday yet, but with a smattering of sun patches still just about breaking through the increasingly dense cloud the Col du Barbier seemed like a fine spot for an early lunch stop and a snooze in the intermittent warmth. Oat bran mixed with raisins, honey and a ground up nut and seed mix has never tasted so good, like sweetened digestive biscuits, and with our bellies feeling very well-looked after we lay back into a patch of soft undergrowth to close our eyes. That I was eating such explosively tasty food on the hillside was partly due to the illness that had laid me low on our Matterhorn tour.

Usually our preferred foods for trekking are fairly repetitive and bland, albeit nourishing and unprocessed. Lentils, pasta, dried fruits, nuts and seeds account for most of what we tended to carry, but after spending more than a week struggling to eat while hiking due to a mouth full of ulcers (and losing a fair bit of weight as a consequence), we'd decided to add honey to the mix and grind up the nuts to make sure I could absorb as much of the fat calories as possible. Not that any of that seemed to matter while I was luxuriating in the pudding-like consistency of it all. We'd started out with enough of the mix for an estimated four days, but it was hard not to scoff the whole bagful immediately.

We dozed for more than an hour in the end, time that passed in the blink of an eye, and we sat up scarcely able to believe my watch. We'd been aware, from time to time, of footsteps and voices but we never expected to sleep so heavily and for so long. While we'd been catching flies the clouds had closed up further, removing any remaining patches of sun to leave an ominous grey blanket that seemed relatively close above our heads.

We began to stretch our sleepy bodies and prepare to start moving again, only to make the happy discovery that we'd been sleeping among an abundance of wild blueberry bushes all the time. We were surrounded by a vast amount of ripe fruit and Esther set straight to work gathering up dozens of plump, purple berries and passing some over to me. Quite why I find the act of actually picking the fruit so tiresome I'm not sure, since I love blueberries, but I'm fortunate that once Esther gets started the process of picking becomes robotic for her. It's getting her to stop that's the challenge!

I joked about Esther's addictive personality and some of her early encounters with eBay in *Just Around The Matterhorn*. Neither of us has ever tried gambling, but let Esther near a push-penny machine on an amusement arcade and you'd better have an extra few pounds handy. It's not the winning that matters (or at least matters that much) but the process. She gets locked into the action and it's exactly the same when picking fruit. "Just one more" is the motto.

We'd been at it for ten minutes or so when we noticed two people approaching who, from fifty metres away, were the spitting image of friends we'd made while motorhome touring a couple of years earlier. Catching each other's eye we both had the same the thought.

"Do you think…" I began.

"It can't be…." replied Esther.

"Well it certainly bloody looks like them…."

It wasn't, of course. It was the young couple we'd noticed packing away their tent back at the Refuge de l'Orgere but because they'd looked identical to some good friends from a distance we felt an immediate affinity with them. That and the fact we were all enjoying the same mountainside and that they were almost certainly hiking the tour of the Vanoise as well (I could see the guidebook sticking out of a pocket – not that I want to suggest I was sizing them up like Benedict Cumberbatch in Sherlock Holmes).

"Do you think they're blueberries?" they asked us, smiling as they approached.

"Well, we hope so now" we replied, "but in seriousness, yes they are." And that is how we started a trend and made some new friends into the bargain, with Renee and Menno from Holland joining us to pick blueberries on the fringe of the Vanoise National Park. The only difference between us was that while we picked hand-to-mouth, delighting in the juicy plumpness of the big ones, Renee was actually saving some in a bottle. Very wise, we thought, continuing to munch until our tongues were bright blue.

After about twenty minutes of companionable picking (and nibbling), the grey sky was starting to worry us a little so we decided we'd better make a start on the remaining three hours of walking outlined in the guidebook. Leaving Renee and Menno still harvesting, we began moving north to skirt the hillside above the two reservoirs nestled below in the Aussois Valley. Passing through undergrowth reminiscent of the Scottish Highlands, the trail continued to slowly rise and fall as it veered inside the park boundary for just a short distance in order to reach another exposed grassy shoulder at 2387 metres. This is the point at which we would have rejoined the main route if we'd chosen to climb straight up from our overnight spot earlier that morning. We were glad we hadn't though as a cloud continued to dominate the col we'd have needed to cross.

With frequent views down to the two reservoirs and the constant presence of countless sheer rock faces peeking at us through the clouds, the park was feeling quite untamed and wild as we began the couple of hundred metres of descending required to cross above a waterfall cascading into the larger of the two reservoirs, the Plan d'Amont. The sky still seemed to be darkening incrementally and it was getting uncomfortably chilly as we half-jogged down towards the water.

Crossing the water via a small bridge, we now left the Vanoise National Park once again and began climbing straight back up towards the Refuge de la Fournache at 2390 metres. There are a total of five separate refuges in the Aussois Valley, so although we'd chosen to go to the one suggested as a stage end point in the guidebook we assumed we had backups if we needed them. That said, when we did arrive at Refuge de la Fournache all we saw was a group of four young lads putting up their tents on the deserted refuge terrace. Evidently the dates given for each refuge in the guidebook weren't always spot on.

It took less than an hour after that to reach the Refuge de Plan Sec, following a flat and wide 4 x 4 track all the way around the hillside until an otherwise unremarkable gap in the undergrowth was singled out with signpost to the refuge. Two minutes later we arrived at an attractive collection of former farm buildings converted into a restaurant and bunkhouses, all occupying a wonderful position above the green Aussois valley. A main dining-room-and-bar cum reception building was flanked by two dormitory buildings, one of which contained toilets and showers, plus another room specifically for camping guests to use. With a series of benches and tables, a sink and a couple of gas rings, it was basically a shared kitchen and dining room for people who wanted to cook their own meals.

Most refuges in the Vanoise National Park are owned and operated by the national park authority (PNV) though a handful of privately owned and managed. The Refuge de Plan Sec at 2350 metres is one such private refuge, with 52 dormitory beds available and a guardian in residence from mid-June to mid-September. Not that we expected or noticed any major difference because it was privately owned. It certainly seemed to have all the key ingredients we'd come to expect from our visits to mountain refuges over the years. A great location, a smiling host, a heavy dose of rustic charm and a mixed-bag of hikers milling around waiting for their dinner. There are, of course, many other variables that characterise different refuges, but it's always the guardian who we find sets the tone in high season. A happy host tends to mean happy hikers and that was our immediate first impression of Refuge de Plan Sec.

The temperature was getting painfully cold by now and the look of the sky meant that even though it was only mid-afternoon the thought of attempting any extra hiking was a foolish one, even for us. We might have been outside of the park boundary at the moment, but if we followed the tour much further we'd soon be back inside and have a very long way to go before we came to the next refuge. No, it looked like it was time for us to break the habit of our summer and actually stop earlier in the day for once. And to get communal with our camping.

We'd mostly wild camped all summer, with just a few hotels thrown in, a couple of deserted cabins and only two campsites. One had been almost empty (in Arolla) and although the one in Zermatt had been undeniably busy, the experience was totally dominated by the heavy engineering works taking place throughout the night nearby.

It wasn't that we'd been anti-social, we'd interacted with plenty of people while passing through and enjoyed their company, but there's always something special to us about being alone with the stars, the dew and the moonlight when night falls. The sense of spaciousness and room to breathe that comes from knowing, beyond the illusion of enclosure that a tent creates, that it's just the two of you lying on a patch of mud and grass, miles from any other person, is priceless to us. We love it. It's why we'd wandered off the night before and camped at the valley head. But for tonight, however, there wasn't another viable option. It was time to get cosy.

Enquiring as to whether we could camp nearby, the friendly owner welcomed us, gave us a tour of the facilities and then showed us the small flat field behind the reception building specifically reserved for tents. There was only one other tent on the field so far, so we had plenty of space to choose from. Ten minutes later we'd popped up our canvas home, unfurled our sleeping gear and were installing ourselves in the kitchen area to keep warm.

Although it obviously wasn't completely rammed yet, from the numbers we could see passing between the various buildings we guessed that at least half of the dormitory guests had already arrived for the evening. Some of the faces we noticed were the same ones we'd seen leaving Refuge de l'Orgere that morning, confirming that even though it was September, the tour (or sections of it) was still a popular route.

Generously, showers were included in the five euros per person bivouacking fee (plus a few cents of tourist tax), so Esther went off to grab hers before the queues got too long. She returned looking warm and satisfied ten minutes later, happily describing how luxuriously warm they were and that they weren't time-limited, as most refuge showers are. She made it sound so delightful that I dashed off eagerly to get my own wash while Esther hung her backup pants out to dry above the dining tables.

Unluckily for me, I left the kitchen and started down the steps to the showers just a third of a second after two other hikers emerged from the dormitory block and beat me to it. A mere second earlier and I'd have been straight in to one of the two empty cubicles for a thorough wash and steam in the blissful warmth. As it was, I found myself mooching around in a cold wooden shed, twiddling my thumbs.

I can't say that I minded waiting too much, at first. It's not like I had somewhere else I urgently needed to be. Still, it took at least five minutes after the doors shut before the shower heads were turned on, and then a further ten minutes of splashing, lathering and splashing again before they were switched off and towels could be heard rubbing away. By this time a decent queue was building up behind me. Inevitably, perhaps unfairly or perhaps understandably depending on your point of view, after twenty minutes of standing in the cold I found my patience wearing thin. A long hot shower at home is one thing, but in a mountain refuge I like to think a certain amount of sympathy and mindfulness towards one's fellow man goes without saying. As does a certain amount of tolerance, of course. That said, occupying the only two shower cubicles for this long was just selfish, or so I'd decided by this point. I was trying really hard not to be annoyed, but the noise of someone going so slowly was taunting me. Like when people don't start bagging up their mountains of shopping at the supermarket until *after* they've paid, but instead just calmly watch it all piling up (take deep breaths Dan, deep breaths).

By the time the first of the two 'spa-goers' emerged in immaculately fresh clothes, smelling of flowers and shining with some sort of sparkly cream, I'd had enough. Naturally, being British I was far too polite to actually say anything, and nor did any of the people in the queue behind me. I just smiled vacantly. Instead, I decided I'd show everyone just how showering should be done.

A friend of mine at university was a member of the Royal Navy and once told me how thirty seconds was considered a long shower on board a ship. Well today I was going for the record. I had no spare clothes with me, or soap, just the damp pack towel that Esther and I were sharing. Jinking into the cubicle I undressed in seconds, leapt under the deliciously hot water for the briefest splash, just enough to get everything wet, towelled myself off vigorously and emerged wearing the same mucky clothes just 75 seconds after the previous occupant had vacated the space. I'd timed it on my watch.

"Plus vite" nodded one gentleman with a grateful nod as I squelched passed him, my bare damp feet jammed into my still sweaty shoes.

"Bravo" exclaimed another with a little clap.

I was gratified to notice as I breezed out past my adoring fans that the other slowcoach was yet to emerge and that their friend was still sprucing themselves up by the sink. I may have foregone the pleasure of long, hot, relaxing shower myself but I'd at least shown the natives how real hikers got clean(ish)! Or idiots. I had the growing feeling that I'd just cut off my nose to spite my face, but what was done was done, so I decided to bask in my rugged smugness for a little while as I went back up for dinner. Esther, by the way, thought I'd been an idiot.

Dinner was a magnificently hot bowl of pasta, which we enjoyed before finding ourselves with unfamiliar time on our hands. What were we supposed to do now? We passed some of our time by flicking through an array of French climbing magazines, marvelling at images of well-muscled people dangling from precarious rock faces. As evening began to fall more faces began to arrive into the dining room, including our Dutch blueberry picking partners Renee and Meno who were also camping here for the night. In total there were about a dozen people camping, mostly young couples, and when I say young what I really mean is younger than us.

Esther was born in Holland, has a Dutch passport and speaks fluent Dutch despite spending most of her childhood in the UK, so it was natural that we fell into conversation with Renee and Menno. They were in their early thirties and were both geologists, which was fantastic because during the past forty-eight hours I'd accumulated a vast stock of random rock-related questions while staring at the intricate and beautiful mountains of the Vanoise. I would have asked them too if it weren't for the fact that the word 'schist' soon crept into the conversation and I found it much more amusing to create as many sentences as possible containing this marvellous word. Anybody listening in might have wondered what the schist was going on? Or maybe I was talking complete schist? To be honest, even if they did, I didn't give a schist.

It turned into a brilliant evening, far more relaxed and laughter-filled than I'd anticipated. The Danish have a word, 'Hygge', which is pronounced 'hue-guh' and roughly translates as cosy with a warm feeling of contentedness, though such a translation doesn't nearly do the word justice. It's a word that has become a little better known since Denmark has been famously floating around the top spots of the annual World Happiness Report in recent years. What's less known is that the Dutch also have a similar word, "gezellig", which means roughly the same thing. And that's exactly what our evening with Renee and Menno was, very gezellig (apart from when poor Menno tried to shower and found that all the hot water had been used up. I told him I knew who was to blame).

Other groups around us were also chatting amicably, creating a warm, family atmosphere as pitch darkness fell outside. Nobody even seemed to notice that mine and Esther's underwear was drying above their heads throughout the evening. We discussed a lot of topics that night, from the environment to politics and a lot of other schist in between. Our companions were interesting, intelligent, well-informed people and we felt very grateful to have met them. They were also, although they were camping, partaking in refuge food which gave us a chance to see how the other half lived.

It turned out to be four-course meal, with soup and bread followed by a big bowl of chilli, then some cake and finally a small cheese platter. It looked delicious and definitely calorie dense enough to sustain a day of hiking. Possibly even two days of hiking. Renee and Menno explained that they did carry some of their own food, but planned to eat mostly refuge breakfasts, lunch bags and dinners during their twelve days of trekking. Unlike us, they weren't keen on descending to resupply, especially as they weren't intending to walk the full Cicerone tour but a combination of the variants and smaller loops specifically so they could spend as much time as possible close to the park's glaciers.

By the time we emerged into the night it was after nine and a dense cloud had encased the refuge buildings, bringing with it a thick drizzle that had plunged the temperature further still. It was no longer just cold, but with the added dampness it was a cold that made any exposed patches of skin sting almost immediately. It took all our strength to manage a flying visit to the toilets before we dived as swiftly as we could into our sleeping bags.

It had been a very different day to anything we'd experienced all summer, particularly spending such a social evening in such excellent company. We'd spent so long steering clear of the busyness of refuges that we'd never really taken the time to contemplate their advantages, but as we lay in our fluffy bags and listened to the drizzle hitting the canvas a few inches from our heads, we began to wonder if the "no bivouacking in the park" rule wouldn't turn out to be a blessing after all.

Vital Statistics – Day 2
Start: Close to Refuge de l'Orgere
End: Refuge de Plan Sec
Distance Hiked: 11 kilometres
Hiking Time: 5 hours
Height Gain: 600 metres
Height Loss: 220 metres

Mist

Daylight bought little respite from the overnight cold and rain that had beaten so relentlessly on our tent, with a vicious wind continuing to drive a dense mist quickly across the hillside when we awoke the next morning. With visibility down to just a few metres, it created a disorientating sense of motion that conflicted with the solid ground beneath us. We packed our sodden tent away with numb fingers, dreaming of the nearby room and the temporary warmth it offered. Fortunately, at this stage of summer, our packing routine was efficient and swift and we didn't have to hang about longer than the few minutes it took us to jam everything loosely into our packs.

A young man without a reservation or a tent had arrived at the already full refuge late the previous evening but the owner, not wanting to turn away a person in need, had found him a spare mattress and laid it out on a table in the salon. So it was a good morning for him as he found himself surrounded by half-soaked campers stringing various soggy possessions around his bed.

For us, it was momentarily gratifying to notice how compact and lightweight our own packs were against the enormous and heavy objects lined up next to them just inside the door. We even lifted a couple to get a sense of the weight and were immediately transported back to the years before we'd invested in some better gear and learned to make do with less. While I continue to have a respect for people carrying such hefty burdens, I honestly wasn't sure I could do it any more, hauling a 20 kilogram (or more) pack for days and weeks on end.

In the past I'd felt proud of the almost immovable object I'd had painfully strapped to myself, convinced it made me tougher than the average hiker, whereas now I just felt a little silly at the memory of myself looking like a bag with legs. That said, I'm sure Esther can think of plenty of current examples of similar silliness, like the week before our Matterhorn tour when I tried to run 105 miles around Mont Blanc without stopping. I'd made it about two thirds of the way before collapsing in a dirty, smelly, hobbling heap in Courmayeur with a bad knee and a dented ego. Still, we live and learn, or at least I try to.

We decided to linger for a short while to see if the weather improved at all, heating up a portion of leftover bean casserole that the refuge owner had kindly provided to Esther for a few euros the night before. It was a remarkably spicy breakfast but an undeniably hot and filling one as we sat gazing out into the seemingly permanent greyness. Two-by-two the other campers hefted their packs and said their farewells, apart from Renee and Menno who were still packing away their own gear and trying to dry their tent a little, a task we'd not even bothered with this time around.

By nine o'clock, with an estimated six hour guidebook stage ahead of us to reach the Refuge de l'Arpont, we decided we couldn't keep waiting and so set out into the mist. If anything the cold seemed to have intensified during our time indoors, growing into an almost physical barrier that knocked us back half a step as we opened the door. The only thing we could do against it was get moving. The guidebook description of the stage waxed lyrical about getting to "experience the true nature of this remarkable region" and "a contrast of high crags dashed with snow and ice", but sadly that was something we could only imagine as we trudged through the mirk.

We knew from our map that we were moving north-east and climbing gently on what appeared to be newly made gravel switchbacks, though the path was surrounded by deep, meandering grooves in the earth. It seemed this was an example of excessive erosion caused by many wandering feet, creating countless criss-crossing options that appeared and vanished around us. We followed the rules and remained on the obvious trail. Even if the weather hadn't made it the only safe option, we would have done so anyway. It was the right thing to do to protect this marvellous park, especially for the sake of a ten second time saving here and there. The sheep didn't though. The air was filled with the muted sound of clonging bells, fading and then growing louder as we snaked and weaved uphill. It seemed we were surrounded by a large herd but we were yet to see a single fluffy animal.

Suddenly, out of the mist, came a great white beast and it definitely wasn't a sheep, charging straight for us and barking. It was a "pastou", a dog who lives permanently with a flock to deter wild animals from attacking the sheep. In this case the red eyes and foaming mouth gave us the good news loudly and clearly. We needed to back off.

Although the breed itself is known as le Montagne des Pyrénées in French, or Great Pyrenees in English, the term "pastou" (pronounced patou) is derived from the word "pastre", literally meaning shepherd in old French. Traditionally, a pastou will have been in contact with sheep from a very early age and from two months old will have been separated from its mother to eat, live and sleep with the sheep it'll be protecting. At the same time, the human shepherd will take care not to caress or provide comfort for the first few years to ensure that the dog's bond is with the sheep and the sheep alone. In short, the sheep are their family and with their large size, thick white coat and floppy ears, they actually blend in very well with the herd. They also look undeniably cute, at least until they bare their teeth.

Despite the slavering mouth and vicious barking, we knew intellectually that the pastou wouldn't actually attack us unless we made aggressive moves towards any of their sisters, the ones we could now see trotting and baaing behind them. They aren't instinctively attack dogs, at least according to what we'd heard from other hikers and read on the information boards dotted around the various mountain regions where they're still used. All it was really trying to do was keep itself between the intruders (us) and its family. We'd seen pastou many times, but only from a distance and had never been warned off like this before.

Fortunately for me, I'm an idiot around dogs and rarely feel intimidated by them, even when they're doing their best to bite me. I'm not sure this is a useful survival trait for a human being to have, but at least it meant I could follow rule number one and stay calm in the face of this big, menacing monster (or cutie pie, as I saw it). Glancing around I could see that its intimidation tactics were definitely working their instinctive magic on Esther, however, so I did my best to keep my own body between her and the pastou as we began a little circling dance routine. In a way the pastou and I were doing the same thing, trying to keep ourselves between the threat and our family, the only difference being I had smaller teeth and opposable thumbs.

We began to walk a wide arc through the mist to try and avoid the sheep as much as we could, but had accidentally bumbled right into the middle of the flock and had sheep popping out of the mist in every direction. In the end we simply continued to walk slowly along the trail, closely shadowed by the still barking dog as I tried to reassure Esther with soothing words, pointing out that if it really wanted to bite us it would already have done so. In hindsight, I'm not sure this was the most reassuring thing I could have said.

The pastou kept trying to go around me to get closer to Esther, but each time it did I stood still and spread my arms wide until it backed off a little, although the metronomic barking never slowed down. It seemed to take ages before we'd passed through all the sheep, not helped by the fact the trail was still zig-zagging and the terrible visibility meant we couldn't simply break off across the hillside in another direction. After about five minutes our barking companion began to quieten down just a little, but still never strayed more than a few metres away from us.

Personally, I was mostly amazed at the dedication and resilience of this incredible animal. I know some people would consider it cruel to leave a dog on the hillside like this while others would think the exact opposite, that it's allowing a dog to actually be a dog and fulfil its instincts. For me, there's no definitive answer, since you could even argue that a 'dog', as opposed to a wolf, is a somewhat human creation thanks to selective breeding etc. But provided there's a shepherd on hand to see the dog is in good health and cared for when necessary, I can only say that the pastou we've seen have looked vibrant and 'relaxed' with their sheep siblings, if a little scruffy. And they do have a very important job to do. We might have been just a couple of flimsy humans with good intentions, but there are much more dangerous predators for these dogs to worry about. The Vanoise, for example, is home to a small number of wolves and although sightings by humans are rare, carcasses of deer and sheep are sometimes found surrounded by wolf tracks.

Back in the early 18th century there were an estimated ten to twenty thousand wolves in France, but they were driven out by a coordinated program of extermination. By the 1930s they had vanished completely. It wasn't until the late 1980s that signs of their return began to appear in the French Alps, probably migrating from nearby parts of the Italian mountains.

Today wolves are a protected species in France, although the estimated population still remains in the hundreds. With wolf packs covering several hundred square kilometres and with their naturally fearful nature, encounters with man are rare, but provided there is enough food there is no reason their numbers won't grow slowly. Hence the use of dogs to deter them from trying to take domestic livestock, the easy targets, instead of deer and wild boar.

After about twenty minutes of canine companionship we began to leave the outlying sheep behind and our furry friend stopped to watch us vanish into the mist. A few minutes after that a scruffy young man with dreadlocks and a couple of collie dogs could be seen coming the other way, looking worried and muttering "Merd" under his breath a lot. He stopped and said something we didn't quite understand but which ended with the word "troupeau", which means flock.

"Are you looking for sheep?" we asked.

"Oui, I have lost my fucking sheep!" he replied in heavily accented English.

We pointed back along the trail. "There are hundreds of sheep about five hundred metres that way." we told him, adding "cinq cent metres" to try and help.

"Merci beaucoup" he exclaimed, looking relieved as he rambled away quickly. Although shepherds do live up on the hillside with their flocks, they don't just sleep on the grass next to them. Most will have a small, temporary hut in the area, a bit like a small shed. Our guess was this bloke had woken up in a cloud and had been wandering around trying to listen out for his flock for some time. The fact he hadn't been able to find them and we hadn't been able to get away seemed rather funny at the time.

Three hours after leaving Refuge de Plan Sec and we still hadn't seen anything we could reasonably describe as scenery. We'd gone up and down a little and had passed a lot of wild blueberry bushes, some of which we'd nibbled at, but after the excitement of the sheep there hadn't been a lot to look at except fog, grass and mud. We'd re-entered the park boundary shortly after setting off and had been traversing around a hillside which our map told us was the flanks of the rugged La Dent Parrachee, the imposing massif we'd gazed at the previous afternoon, but it wasn't until we began a short descent back towards the park boundary that we suddenly dropped out of the cloud. That's also when it started to rain.

After a slippery descent down some smooth stone steps chiselled into the mountain, we propped ourselves in the doorway of a dilapidated barn and weighed up our options. It was about one o'clock, it was raining fairly hard and we could feel the cold and dampness of the past few hours weighing heavy in our limbs. We estimated we only had about another ninety minutes of mostly flat walking to reach the Refuge de l'Arpont at the end of the stage, and we definitely had no intention of trying to go any further than that today. But we were also tired right now and in need of a pause, despite the cold.

The next thing we knew, we were waking up to find Renee and Menno waving at us from the nearby trail and asking if we were okay. We hadn't planned to doze, but sleep had crept up on us unnoticed and left us drooling on each other's shoulder for the past half an hour or more. We assured Renee and Menno that we weren't dead yet and began rubbing our stiff arms legs to get them ready for the final approach.

We began walking again, now beneath the low blanket of cloud which at least allowed us to see into the damp green valley beneath us. We were once again tracking the park boundary, looking down into the village of Termignon where two years earlier we'd spent an October's night in our motorhome on the way to cycle up the Col de l'Iseran. It felt strange to be looking down on the clearly outlined parking bay we'd slept in from so far above. I mean, to think of all that had happened since we'd arrived in that distant place with a gaggle of seven-month-old puppies on board was a really humbling experience. What adventures we'd had and were continuing to be blessed with.

It was a very soggy and cloud-covered traverse that came next, heading around the Combe d'Enfer beneath the unseen glaciers now above us. Snaking through rough pastures and close to engorged waterfalls, we were pleased that Renee and Menno were ahead of us because they kept stopping to photograph the larger cascades as they thundered over wet black rocks. Their frequent stops reminded us that after so many weeks of walking, we'd perhaps become a little de-sensitised to the subtle beauty of the immediate hillside when the grander spectacles of snow-capped summits were hidden. Watching them appreciating all of the little things gave us a nudge not to take anything for granted.

A few metres to the side of the trail a small group of sheep were trying to shelter from the rain, huddling behind a half-collapsed wall with a pastou dozing quietly at the centre of the white mass and using a nearby sheep as a pillow. The dog opened one lazy eye to watch us as we walked quietly past, but this one didn't bother standing up, preferring instead to keep its large head on its sister's back.

The Refuge de l'Arpont was originally built in the early 1970s but was completely refurbished in 2017, so was still looking new and shiny when we arrived. With a magnificent position just a few hundred metres below the tongue of the Glacier de l'Arpont, it has 94 beds available in a large bunkhouse and even includes a handful of private double rooms. In many ways, it's a bastion of modernity hidden within a respectfully traditional design.

We checked in, paying the five euros per person bivouac fee and being directed to a fenced-off, irregularly shaped area outside, about a twenty-five metre walk away. We were the first tent to arrive so had our pick of places, which was good because we couldn't find a single genuinely flat spot anywhere. Eventually we settled on what seemed like the least sloping square of earth, even though it had a two inch wide trench running through it, and pitched our tent and sleeping gear before taking everything else back inside to dry off.

Like Refuge de Plan Sec, Refuge de l'Arpont also has a separate salon for guests not staying in the main dormitory, in addition to a vast, humid and rather aromatic drying room that was already crammed with waterproofs, boots and dripping packs. Retrieving our stove and some food, we slid our packs into a corner, slipped out of our muddy shoes and into a nice dry pair of refuge-supplied crocs. Unfortunately, warm showers weren't included this time around and nor was use of the gas stove in the salon, but we didn't feel we really needed either and were content to just sit at the end of the long bench and warm up. If anything the salon was too warm due to the roaring wood-burner right at the centre of the room, but after spending six hours in the cold and rain we weren't going to complain as we peeled off our mid-layers and began thawing out. Across the corridor we could see the main dining area and reception desk, busy with a steady stream of visitors checking in, paying for the meals they'd be having later or otherwise just sitting and staring out of the windows.

A few others ventured into the salon but tended to wander out again quickly, giving just a tiny sense of a divide between the dormitory guests and those of us setting up our camping stoves on the long wooden table. By early evening there were about a dozen of us again, although Renee and Menno were the only faces we recognised from the night before. Once again the atmosphere was warm and hospitable, everyone politely dancing around each other as they passed in and out or waited to use the sink. There was no tension or rush, just a sense of a transient family that had come together for a single night, united in our common love of the outdoors and our choice to visit the Vanoise on this particular day. Despite at least five different languages being spoken, including English, French, German, Italian and Dutch, the conversation managed to flow freely up and down the table thanks to the fact that most people spoke more than one language and were happy to chip in with a little translation help here and there. It was certainly a far cry from sitting in a cold, wet tent waiting for darkness to fall on an otherwise foul weather hiking day.

By the time we did venture outside to bed it was pitch dark and the cloud had closed in again, leaving our new headtorches casting their light into fog so thick we could hardly see our own feet. But it was just enough to find our tent and bring another day of new experiences to an end. Hopefully it would brighten up by morning?

Vital Statistics – Day 3
Start: Refuge de Plan Sec
End: Refuge de l'Arpont
Distance Hiked: 18 kilometres
Hiking Time: 6 hours
Height Gain: 520 metres
Height Loss: 350 metres

Off Plan

Another cold, zero-visibility morning greeted us, with both our outer and inner tent soaked with dew. Although it was a long shot, we decided to change our morning routine slightly and just leave our tent up on the slim chance that this was just a morning mist and would burn off shortly. Instead, we picked our way through the tall, wet grass back to the refuge where the bulk of our gear was waiting for us in the drying room.

We knew from Renee and Menno, who had signed up for the refuge breakfast, that the meal had started at 6.30 a.m., so it was unsurprising to find the refuge largely empty when we arrived an hour later. Most of the dormitory guests seemed to have either already left or were in the final stages of lacing their boots and collecting their lunch packs from the dining room. We knew our friends hadn't left yet though as we'd heard them packing away their tent.

A small number of other campers were already at the salon table, so we slid onto the end to prepare some oatbran, nuts and honey from our now visibly dwindling supplies. We soon fell into conversation with a group of four hikers, two French, one Swiss and one Italian, who were friends from university spending a week in the Vanoise. Clement spoke the best English and with his long hair and flowing beard, he looked a little like a well-groomed Viking. Like us, he was toting a DIY muesli mix and began lamenting how "bed factories", as he called them, like this refuge were forced to offer up so much long-life cheese and processed meat for breakfast, but not a single piece of fruit. "It's the only way they can feed almost 100 people every night, but it's just so clinical here." he said. "Some of the smaller refuges make you feel so welcome, but here you're just a warm body and a handful of euros passing through."

Personally, we could see his point but also understood that the refuge had little choice. The bigger the refuge, the more people it can support to be in this fantastic region, but the more it must necessarily lose the individual touch. And besides, how could we complain when we were sitting here benefitting from that lovely wood burning stove? For me, given the choice, I'd take a big bed factory over no refuge at all. Like many things in life, it's all about managing expectations.

After some food and a comforting saucepan of tea, we unfurled our map and opened the guidebook to weigh up our options. For two days now we'd followed the "Tour of the Vanoise" guidebook itinerary without question, deterred from any major detours partly by our intention to stick to the plan, but mostly by the bad weather and the lack of any real options to take alternative routes. We'd been basically heading east along the park boundary for two days and the only real option to walk deeper inside the park so far would have taken us straight back through it towards Pralognan.

Today, however, there was a choice. The next guidebook stage to the Refuge du Plan du Lac was a five hour horseshoe completely within the park boundaries and was described as one of "the great walks of the tour", with "tremendous views practically every step of the way".

Unfortunately, looking out of the window into a grey blankness, we doubted that would be our own experience. After that, a further two stages continued to snake eastwards, returning to and then hugging the park boundary above the Maurienne Valley to reach the village of Bonneval-sur-Arc, before the route cut north in a stage that reached the ski-town of Val d'Isere. In many ways, those three stages together closely matched the road up and over the Col de l'Iseran that we'd cycled.

Studying the descriptions of the four stages directly ahead, provided the weather cleared up, we'd no doubt be in for a variety of rich treats as we hiked. However, looking at our map, we couldn't help feeling that we might prefer an alternative route to reach Val d'Isere, one that went directly through the heart of the park and away from the road entirely.

The most obvious choice was via the Vallon de la Rocheure, with a night at the Refuge de la Femma on the way. This was actually included in the guidebook as a recommended detour for those who had an extra day in hand to explore it. Yet while the guidebook proposed visiting the Refuge de la Femma, staying overnight and then doubling back to the main route, our map showed that we could just as well continue up the valley to cross the 2911 metre Col de la Rocheure and then descend straight into Val d'Isere. It would mean cutting two days off the main guidebook route, two days we'd have to find something useful to do with, but it was an exciting prospect to take a route entirely cut off from the world of roads and civilisation. Oh well, so much for just sticking to the itinerary and taking it easy! It was definitely exciting though.

So we had a new plan, all we had to do now was brace ourselves for another day of chilly dampness. A weather forecast pinned up in the main refuge dining room suggested we had at least another couple of cold days on the way before the sun 'might' return, but even then the long-term forecast remained unsettled. And besides, as a very intelligent friend of ours who spent his entire career working for the Met' Office as a forecaster had once explained to us, even the most detailed weather models are mostly just informed guesses after more than forty-eight hours. The weather is just too complex to predict micro-effects like rain, cloud and sun within a few kilometres. Macro-scale climate models, on the other hand, only point in one direction. "There is no climate debate among scientists anymore" he told us, "there hasn't been for years."

It was the same message we'd heard from Renee and Menno, whose geological work with ice cores told the same story. We're not just in a warm spell of global climate history, they'd told us definitively, we're in a phase where temperatures are rising faster than ever before due to human activity, and are set to continue rising faster still due to the accelerating nature of various feedback loops. Take ice, for example. It's white and so reflects the heat of the sun, but as the polar ice caps melt that's less 'white stuff' to do the reflecting. On the other hand, as temperatures rise there might also be more clouds which can at least reflect some heat, which is why the precise rate of future warming is so hard to predict, an uncertainty some climate change deniers pounce on to claim the scientists are "unsure", about both the size of the effect and the cause. But in reality the trend is one way only and it's down to us, requiring swift and drastic lifestyle and industrial changes to prevent enormous human and animal suffering around the world. I remember discussing which generation will feel the suffering first with my well-informed meteorologist friend, and he looked at me with a frown and said "Dan, I'm sorry to say, but it's going to be in your lifetime, long before you're an old man".

Of course, this is just my layman's summary of some very interesting conversations with far better-informed people, but it was a chilling thought that all of the beauty we liked to surround ourselves with in places like the Vanoise could change beyond recognition in a matter of years. All while politicians continue to dither or outright backtrack on emissions legislation as they bow to the short-term demands of interest groups who just want to make more money. Or, worse still, peddle propaganda that has sections of the public also crying "climate hoax", "it's only because they want to raise taxes" or (my personal favourite) "tell that to China!", as if pointing out that other countries are still polluting is a solid argument for continuing to pollute ourselves. What's wrong with setting a good example and leading in clean technology? And that includes member of the public who can afford to choosing utilities or products that have a cleaner energy footprint, even if they're a little more expensive.

Rant over, this isn't a book about climate politics (although in a way it is since it's a book about the beauty of nature and the two are irrevocably linked together). Back in the Vanoise and Refuge de l'Arpont, we retrieved our packs from beneath the shelves in the drying room, dropped down our tent, bought it in from the mist to roll away in the warm and layered-up ready to set out.

By now the refuge staff were hoovering and cleaning up around us, since pretty much everyone else had already left for the day, and that's when we spotted a little rabbit hopping around in the dining room. For more than a decade, back in our old lives, we'd enjoyed free roaming house-rabbits lolloping around our home. I think it's become more well-known nowadays that rabbits make excellent house pets. They're sociable, litter train naturally and provided they aren't grabbed or startled, can really enjoy human companionship and fuss. At first, it had taken me a while to come around to the idea myself, but what had finally melted my heart was a crazy-haired, floppy-eared bundle of softness we called Thumper. Never before had I encountered a rabbit who sought out human contact so much. He followed us around, sat and watched us on the loo and even at night-time he was ever alert to the chance he might get some attention. All we had to do was dangle an arm out of the edge of our bed and within seconds we'd hear him hopping across the room to nuzzle his head under our fingers. Needless to say, we couldn't possibly leave the refuge without fussing the rabbit.

In the end we left at half past nine, the very last guests to go, and began striding through the cloud. Our immediate route would take us beneath the vastness of the Glaciers de la Vanoise as we moved north on the western flank of the Doron de Termignon valley. If we could have seen anything, which we couldn't, we would have been gazing towards the two giants of the Vanoise, La Grande Casse (3855 m) and La Grande Motte (3653 metres), and the sharp ridgeline that connects them to create an enormous amphitheatre of rock and ice.

Thankfully, as we walked the mist did begin to thin out a little, gradually opening up our field of view to at first a few tens of metres and then, after an hour so, to a few hundred metres either side of us. Crossing streams and skirting by small glacial lakes, we even began to get occasional hints of higher ice fields and blue sky until, all of a sudden, the mist seemed to shoot away from us and we found ourselves in a beautiful bowl formed of rough green hillside, dark lakes, darker rock and bright white glacial flows. The remaining clouds above us were now stretched out in long thin streams, cutting across the blue, while curtains of mist continued to extend down into the valley like the ghosts of waterfalls.

Having started out with such low expectations for the scenic side of the day, this was a real treat that we'd been completely unprepared for. Which is why, after the previous couple of hours of plodding through the moody bleakness, we decided not to miss the opportunity and found a comfy boulder to rest on for a while. We even got our soaking tent out for twenty minutes to dry a little in the occasional sun patches drifting across the ground.

We were now tucked beneath the brown spire-like cliffs of Mont Pelve, with a sliver of the Glacier du Pelve just visible beyond a black-surfaced glacial lake surrounded by grey boulders deeply embedded in the moist earth. Even during the thirty minutes we spent resting, the weather continued to fluctuate quickly between overcast autumnal gloom and summertime loveliness. It was like visiting this wondrous scene at two different times of year simultaneously.

After our magical little pause we continued to traverse, passing beneath Mont de la Para to reach a path junction overlooking the confluence of three valleys, the Doron de Termignon valley that we'd been walking above so far today, the Vallon de la Rocheure that we intended to take next, and the more northerly Vallon de la Leisse, along which the tour of the Vanoise would return after passing through Val d'Isere.

It was a magnificent outlook, with the melancholy clouds hovering above parts of each valley suggesting a stormier afternoon might yet lie in store, despite the locally brightening sky. The wide and flat-bottomed Vallon de la Rocheure stretched towards a dark wall of rock at its head, while we could only see the mouth of the Vallon de la Leisse. It was only a kilometre or so away from us, we could have cut across to it in just quarter of an hour, so it was strange to think that the conventional tour route took more than a week to return that way.

It was while surveying these adjacent valleys that we caught up with Renee and Menno, themselves enjoying a pause in the lee of a house-sized boulder. They'd had a fantastic time beneath the Glaciers de la Vanoise and were themselves now weighing up their route options. They too didn't feel inclined to race around the park boundary to Val d'Isere but also preferred the idea of lingering in this heart of the park beneath its highest peak. We explained our plan to head to Refuge de la Femma while they reviewed the various refuge details in their own copy of the Cicerone guide.

Renee, it seemed, had an almost photographic memory of the route having studied the guide in detail for several weeks, a memory which emphasised our own sketchy suck-it-and-see approach to planning on the fly. In the end they narrowed it down to either going to Refuge de la Femma themselves, or cutting across to the Vallon de la Leisse and climbing up to the Refuge de la Leisse instead.

61

We left them debating, wishing them well and hoping that we'd see them again soon, whatever they decided.

A swift descent into the head of the Doron de Termignon valley followed, stopping every now and then to harvest more handfuls of succulent blueberries, before we joined a tarmac road heading uphill and eastwards into the Vallon de la Rocheure. We had only a few hundred metres of climbing to reach the Refuge de la Femma, but at least six kilometres of trekking along the smoothly rising valley. The sun continued to tease us, cooking us and making us sweat as we power-marched up the tarmac towards a handful of farms, but then vanishing to leave us cold and damp as we stepped back onto the gravel road that continued further up-valley.

If there was a defining characteristic of Vallon de la Rocheure that day, it was marmots. Hundreds and hundreds of them were galloping across the flat and green valley floor either side of the track, most of them chirruping a warning before diving into a burrow as we approached. A handful, however, were less nervous and were content to just watch us warily as we passed within just a few metres of them and the mouth of their den. Some even seemed to be showing off, standing up on their rear legs and displaying their bulging tummies for us to inspect.

Marmots in the Alps can hibernate from as early as October, so these fellows were possibly in their final few weeks of fattening up before a long winter sleep. Sealed up in their burrows, huddled together for warmth, their heart rate drops to just a few beats per minute as they rely on stored fat to survive the long cold winter. With so many marmots around it can be easy to take them for granted, but they are fascinating animals in their own right. Perfectly adapted to an ice age climate, they can burrow into earth that would worry a pick-axe and survive on a diet of grass, insects, spiders and worms. Barring injury, winter starvation or being hunted, this largest of the squirrel species can live over 15 years! Although it's tempting to imagine a marmot utopia underground (I know I have), with so many near-identical marmots dashing into thousands of nearby burrow openings, most marmots actually live in a small group with a limited number of burrows and a dominant breeding pair.

They are also definitely not pets, as cute as they are, and we'd often seen signs warning visitors not to feed the marmots. Just like humans, junk food can cause them to get skin conditions like eczema and psoriasis, or give them diarrhoea and other digestive issues. Personally, having seen the size of their front teeth up close, I wouldn't fancy trying to feed a marmot at all, even if one got close enough to try.

Nevertheless, our passage up the long Vallon de la Rocheure was marked by the constant warnings of fleeing marmots plus a short doze in the wind-shelter of a tiny chapel, during which time Renee and Menno passed us again! We woke up just in time to see their packs vanishing into the green, cloud-covered opening ahead of us. It was almost becoming a farce now, how we kept leap-frogging each other. But in a way, it made us feel that much closer to them, even after just three days of friendship. We were definitely pleased they'd chosen the same route as us for an extra day, even though we knew it would probably be our last evening with them.

By the time we reached the Refuge de la Femma we were once more in front, arriving at a three-storey wooden house flanked by a pair of single-level pointy-roofed bunkhouses, the whole enclosed by a fence and nestled beneath a small cliff. The first to greet us was a white-coated mule who came trotting up to the gate to say hello and get a cuddle. She was wonderfully friendly and held us up for a good ten minutes with her nuzzling attentions until we finally slipped inside to request a campsite for the night.

We were met inside by Elsa who was busy baking some sort of enormous chocolate pie for the evening guests.

She was expecting only seven people who had reserved for the evening, she explained, so it was going to be a much quieter night than we had grown used to at our previous two refuges. Pointing outside, she told us that we could pay our five euro bivouac fee later and were welcome to camp anywhere just the other side of the fence. We could also, if we wanted, make use of the showers upstairs or the kitchen area at the other end of the clean, large dining area we were stood in. She made us feel very welcome and at home, also explaining how this was a 100% organic food refuge which we thought was brilliant. Méane, the mule, usually helped to bring up the supplies from the road head, although they did still use helicopter deliveries from time to time.

Our own food supplies were quite low by this point, so we asked if we might buy a little muesli, or similar, from her and perhaps a little fruit to supplement our meals until we could get to Val d'Isere the next day. She told us she didn't have much spare food, but did give us a 250 gram bag of buckwheat flakes, two quite shrivelled apples and offered me a bowl of rice at dinnertime, if I wanted it? We did consider joining the evening meal properly, but she told us it was lamb stew and so it rather ruled it out for two non-meat eaters like us. A bowl of rice would do nicely though.

Our tent was half up when Renee and Menno arrived, so we explained what we'd learned inside and that we were happy to have their company for a third night in a row.

What followed was another very pleasant evening, though it started cold. Esther and I dashed excitedly upstairs for a quick shower only to discover that they actually required a token. We didn't realise until we were naked though, so braved an icy rinse off before handwashing our four-day old socks and salt-stained hiking tops in the bathroom sink to hang up above the wood-burner at the centre of the dining room.

As darkness began to fall, the other seven guests arrived, and as we cooked our penultimate portion of pasta, everyone else sat down to their lamb nearby. Elsa, as promised, bought me a small portion of white rice to top up my own dinner. To be honest, I was quite full by then, but ate it anyway. Unfortunately, the apples had proved to be rotten inside.

Meals finished, we played a Dutch card game called klaverjassen with Renee and Menno, a four-person game of trumps played with two teams of two. It's a game that holds a very dear place in our hearts as it's the game we would always play with Esther's grandparents on our various visits to see them in Holland. Before I could speak even a single word of Dutch, I had learned to play klaverjassen and would join in with the good-natured laughter, competition and outwardly ridiculous 'rituals' associated with a run of bad luck, such as Esther's Opa (grandfather) dancing around his chair to change his fortunes (which usually worked by the way). Since Opa had passed away eight years earlier, we'd hardly played a hand, so it was a special moment that we got to play it out here in our beloved wilderness.

I can't say any of us was that handy any more, and it took us a little while to discover the 'Utrecht' version of the game that Renee and Menno knew was a little different to the version Esther and I had played with her grandparents, but we at least laughed more than we had in weeks. I'd say I can't remember who won, but only because it was Renee and Menno.

The only small stain on what was otherwise a perfect evening came when we went to pay our bill and found ourselves on the hook for over thirty euros. Ten plus a few cents was our camping fee, but it turned out we were being asked for five euros for the two apples, five euros for the small bowl of rice, five for the buckwheat flakes and another three euros each for using the kitchen. Renee and

Menno, who had both showered and ordered a lunch bag and breakfast, were only paying just over fifty.

We each felt a little indignant at first but we had little choice but to pay. The mistake was ours for not checking prices before accepting the items and for assuming that no sign in the kitchen meant it was included, as it had been back at the Refuge de Plan Sec. By making our 'off-menu' requests it was really a case of Elsa making something up on the spot, and with a refuge to support she had simply erred on the high side. We could see her point of view, once we'd got over the shock, but it did remind us to check refuge prices in advance from now on. This time we just had to put it down to experience and consider it a donation to the upkeep of this wonderful and remote refuge, which isn't a shop and does have significant overheads when it comes to deliveries.

It was another bitterly cold night outside as we went back to our tents. Renee had told us several times during the evening that it was forecast to snow and that it was supposed to reach minus three degrees overnight, an exciting prospect really. We were well over two thousand metres and with possible snow forecast, we could well be waking up in a winter wonderland.

Vital Statistics – Day 4
Start: Refuge de l'Arpont
End: Refuge de la Femma
Distance Hiked: 19 kilometres
Hiking Time: 5 hours
Height Gain: 620 metres
Height Loss: 570 metres

Luxury

Renee was right, it did snow in the night and it was still snowing when the morning light began to seep through the walls of our tent. From our warm sleeping bags we could hear the hissing-scratching sound of small snowflakes sliding down the outside of the canvas as we lay enjoying our morning cuddle. "What adventures do you think we'll have today?" we asked each other, as usual, both elated with the idea it was actually snowing outside.

When we did brave the cold and left our sleeping bags, we hurried into our semi-frozen hiking clothes and popped our heads outside to find ourselves looking out onto a world tinged with white. It wasn't a deep, thick snow that had fallen, at least not at this altitude, but a light dusting that half-covered most surfaces. Unfortunately, during one of my nocturnal toilet trips in the night, it seemed I'd failed to tuck my shoes back into the shelter of my little porch area and so they were now full of snow. Fortunately, because it was so cold, I was able to bang most of it out before slipping them on and standing up to stretch in the crisp air.

As we'd done at Refuge de l'Arpont, we'd left our bags in the boot room overnight so we simply unpegged our tent and carried it still erect over to the refuge to fold away with the rest of our gear. It may have been snow-covered but it was at least mostly dry once we'd given it a good shake. We still spread it out in the boot room though, to dry a little more, while we headed upstairs to the dining room for a warm breakfast of lentil pasta with curry spices. We had planned to have porridge, but looking at the snow coming down outside we knew we'd be unlikely to enjoy cooking pasta outside at lunchtime. Instead, we decided to keep our last few oats for a simple trail snack, pre-mixing them with a little water and honey to save time in the cold later on.

Our plan for the day had been to cross the 2911 metre Col de la Rocheure and descend into Val d'Isere, but with the grey sky and the continuing snow we were wondering if that was still such a sensible plan after all? Renee and Menno had already told us they'd changed their own route in response to the weather. They'd been planning to navigate a 2800 metre pass directly over to the Refuge de la Leisse but were now going to head back down the valley and take a lower altitude option.

In the end we decided to chance it. It was 'only' an extra 600 metres higher than our current position and the weather could go either way. It might close in and become a blizzard, but it might not. The forecast provided by Elsa was inconclusive. Besides, unless we got to Val d'Isere we wouldn't be able to resupply with food and would be dependent on refuge meals. Our pre-mixed oats represented the very last of our own food, at least until we got to a shop.

We wished Renee and Menno a happy and safe onward journey in what was a rare and slightly emotional farewell for us. We'd met and spoken to many people during our adventures but it was uncommon for us to spend more than a single evening with any one person or group. Having enjoyed three consecutive evenings with a couple who shared so many of our interests, combined with the additional shared experience of the trails we'd walked, had made us feel very comfortable and happy in their company. While there are many wonderful features of a nomadic life, it's undeniable that the closeness of nearby, long-term friends is something that we occasionally miss, which is what we'd briefly enjoyed again for the previous three evenings. But then the door closed on the snow and we were alone once more, just the two of us, standing in an empty dining room with a hill to climb.

We lingered a little longer in the quiet of the refuge, passing the time by watching the snow and pedalling on the exercise bike in the centre of the dining room. Unlike other refuges, there were no power points for use by guests and this was the only way to charge electronic devices. I put about quarter of an hour into our camera while we waited and watched the sky, trying to discern if it would brighten at all?

As the time approached ten o'clock, we decided we couldn't wait anymore and stepped out onto the snow-covered terrace surrounding the refuge. The wind was blowing powerfully from the south, our right-hand side, whipping the small icy flakes hard across our cheeks as we shuffled our heads back as far as we could into the hoods of our waterproofs. Visibility was mediocre at best, perhaps 100 metres at times but often a lot less. We were going up, we knew that, we just couldn't always see where we were going. A sign close to the refuge suggested we were two hours from the top of the col, so provided we could make out the trail we hoped it would go smoothly. Failing that, we had a compass.

The ground was frozen beneath our feet as we weaved our way through the semi-snow-covered landscape, leaning into the wind as we gradually gained height. Beneath my mid-layers and waterproofs I could feel sweat beginning to bead on my back, but it was far too cold to think about losing any layers just yet. To be honest, I liked the sense of danger and wildness that the foul weather cast across the park. There we no footprints in the snow even, as though we were pioneers in an unexplored land.

But then it all began to change. You could say that our gamble had paid off, I suppose, as the snow eased and the mist began to fade away, slipping up the surrounding valley head like a receding tide. Yet there was a part of me that was a little disappointed.

Within an hour of leaving the refuge we could see the entire broad white amphitheatre of the valley head, with the snow and the occasional dark patches beneath overhangs emphasising the undulating contours, crags and cliffs. We were rising up the northern side of the bowl and fairly soon there were even a few patches of blue sky above us. Several small glaciers could now be made out on our right, appearing as pristine fields of unbroken whiteness that flowed down from the slopes of the highest peak on the valley ridgeline, the Pointe de Mean Martin at 3330 metres.

Although it had stopped snowing, the covering that had already settled wasn't going anywhere soon. As we climbed the snow beneath our feet continued to get deeper until, as we approached the col itself, we were leaving several-inch deep footprints in the virgin snow. It was a delightful feeling as our shoes pressed into the flakes, each footstep making a sound like old floorboards creaking gently in the night.

We reached the Col de la Rocheure easily enough in the end, arriving at a snowy saddle next to the black surface of the Lac de la Rocheure, from where we gazed out over the empty, wintery wilderness we'd trekked through. Although the weather had improved markedly, an inhospitable wind could now be felt blowing strongly from the other side of the col, which is why we decided it was wise to eat our oats right away since we were unlikely to want to stop on the way down into Val d'Isere.

Perched on a small, icy cairn, we held each other closely and marvelled at the incredible place our bodies had taken us to. It was like having our own frozen palace of pinnacles to enjoy for a few short moments. Every now and then the wind would die down, smoothing the surface of the lake into a mirror which reflected the icy tundra for just a handful of special seconds.

The cold motivated us to move on sooner than we might otherwise have done, it being such an idyllic winter scene. However, we'd at least had a small taste of it and we'd done enough hiking over the years to be grateful for that. We knew that the weather could have easily gone the other way and left us lost in the clouds.

We began our descent with a quick jog down some icy switchbacks and out onto a bleak plateau of dark scree that soon gave way to damp pastures. The blue skies that had briefly opened up had now vanished, with freezing fog filled with light rain now closing in to leave us feeling chilled to the bone. Esther, in particular, had rapidly lost all sensation in her hands and couldn't even hold her trekking poles any more. Sadly, our feet didn't quite lose all sensation and just hurt.

We'd been struggling with our new shoes ever since we began our first descent on day one. They'd been fine on all of the uphill sections, but whenever we'd gone downhill the tops of our feet had pressed uncomfortably into the laces, eyelets and tongue of the shoe, leaving both of us with dark bruises. That the problem was basically the same for each of us, the only difference being the exact position of the bruising, had convinced it was something to do with the design of the shoe. We'd worn Salomon boots and trail running shoes before, always finding them unfalteringly comfortable, so I don't mean to disparage the brand. But in this case we were much less happy, each of us wearing the same model of shoe and having the same problems.

On day one it had been a mild chafing accompanied by a worrying sense that we might have made an unwise choice. On the subsequent three days the pain had remained an ever present companion, but because there hadn't been too much downhill it had been manageable. All we'd had to do was leave our laces slightly undone to try and minimise the pressure on the bruises. Mostly, that had worked, although Esther now had some worryingly large swellings. We'd even done our best to laugh it off for the previous four days, but now the combination of the icy cold plus a continuous, 1100 metre descent finally threatened to break our resilience to the pain.

"Fucking piece of shit shoes" I shouted at the wind as I loosened my own wire-like laces completely in an attempt to remove even the tiniest hint of pressure from the battered tops of my feet. "Of course wearing brand new shoes on a multi-day hike was always going to be a bad fucking idea!" I really had hoped that the trainer-like design would mean there was no 'breaking in' required, not like the chunky boots I'd had to buy in Zermatt during our Matterhorn tour that had cut my heels to pieces for the following week.

Wincing with each step and writing a scathing, swear-word peppered review in my head (which I'd never actually post), we half-jogged, half-limped down the winding and frozen descent towards Val d'Isere. We did get a little light relief in the form of a herd of cows that were stood in the frozen mud partway down, the funny part being that one cow looked almost exactly like UK Prime Minister Boris Johnson. On each side of him stood two mini-herds. One herd contained only white cows, the other only brown. Clearly bovine Boris was a divisive leader of 'udders' (Get it! I said *udders*... Never mind).

After two hours of numb-faced, sore-footed descending we arrived on the outskirts of Val d'Isere and began hobbling in the direction we hoped would lead us to both food and shelter. Val d'Isere is one of the better-known ski resorts in the Alps, an ever-expanding collection of hotels, apartment complexes and ski lifts stretching for a couple of kilometres either side of the D902 road about 12 kilometres before it gets to the lofty Col de l'Iseran.

During the 1992 Albertville Winter Olympic, Val d'Isere was the location for several skiing events and it still annually hosts World Cup skiing contests. With over 300 kilometres of pistes and 78 ski-lifts in the area, it's no surprise the tourist office claimed over 1 million "ski boots on dance floors" for the 2017/18 ski season. Yet it's also a popular summer destination due to the fact it happens to be right on the doorstep of the Vanoise National Park.

We'd passed through Val d'Isere a couple of times before, on bikes and in our motorhome. Both times, from above, we'd been struck by the stark contrast between the surrounding untouched hillsides and the sprawling mass of ugly buildings in what would otherwise be a stunning Alpine valley. This time around we felt similarly, especially after the total lack of development in the park itself. However, while it may not be totally in keeping with the nearby national park, there's no denying that this particular ski-town opens up the breathtaking scenery to a large number of people. Plus, ski towns do just look better when covered in a thick layer of powder snow instead of persistent wet sleet.

The biggest surprise on this particular visit, however, wasn't the industrialisation but the almost completely deserted streets and closed-for-the-season hotel buildings. It was only early September for crying out loud. Where was everybody? It might have been a chilly day, but even so, surely there should have been thousands of visitors and restaurants thronging with hungry customers. The only human presence we could see were a few cold looking builders slowly moving materials around a handful of half-built apartment buildings.

We'd started the day intending to get to town, grab supplies and check in to the campsite, but this unanticipated deadness told us that perhaps it wasn't going to be quite so simple. Indeed, a quick web search on Esther's phone (now that we were back in the world of mobile data) revealed that the campsite had already closed for the year and that all of the supermarkets but were one were closed until December, that one being also shut until Monday morning. In other words, no grub until tomorrow.

Locating the tourist office, which also just so happened to be closed for lunch, we realised that we needed a new plan. The temperature was already just a few degrees above zero and although the rain had currently stopped, a forecast in the tourist office window suggested that it was going to be -5°C overnight. We were tired, sore-footed and chilled to our core. It was time to get a room.

In previous books I've mentioned our historic issues about forking out for pricey rooms when we wanted to be 'hardcore' hikers, but in this instance there really wasn't any other sensible option. In many ways it wasn't even a choice. Sure, we could have 'survived' a night in our tent in a nearby frozen field, but even we could see that would be suffering for the sake of it. A quick browse of Booking.com revealed that only two hotels were open in the whole of Val d'Isere, both with a spa and both for a similar price at just over 100 euros. It was more than we would have liked to spend, but then again it seemed we had little choice in the matter.

Both hotels turned out to be within easy walking distance of the tourist office, so we took a stroll to each one before opting for the Hotel Avancher, a modern, plush-looking hotel with excellent customer reviews online. Our five days of hiking so far had been made infinitely easier by being able to spend the past three evenings in the warmth of a refuge, rather than on cold grass outside of our tent, but the sudden necessity of an actual hotel room was a beguiling prospect, an unexpected treat that I was suddenly hungry to dive into.

We checked in smoothly, despite our ragged appearance, and I knew we were both giddy with the excitement of an unplanned night of opulence and cleanliness. Keycards in hand, we practically sprinted up to our third floor room where we discovered a magnificent nest of comfort, with a huge double bed, balcony and a swanky bathroom with a massive two-person bath.

Everything was finished to such a wonderfully high standard that we almost couldn't believe they had let two filthy, trail-stained hikers like us into the place.

Twenty minutes later we were walking happily barefoot along the hotel's corridors in search of the spa, wearing nothing but our still wet, hand-washed underwear beneath the thick white dressing gowns supplied in our room. Everything around us seemed newly decorated, including the immaculate spa that contained a raised jacuzzi set against a completely glass wall looking out over the hills, a pristine steam room and a fresh-pine sauna set to one side. But the best part was the "Stairway to Heaven". Not that Led Zeppelin's masterpiece was being played in the background (though it would have been nice), but the additional sauna on the roof that was accessed via a short staircase, hence the name. The outdoor sauna itself was like a huge wine-cask tipped on its side, with a transparent cap on one end that directed the view straight onto the surrounding slopes. We may have been summer guests, but with the foul weather continuing we could easily imagine what a welcome delight this would be after a cold day on skis, or in our case, a cold day in painful shoes.

We ended up spending a couple of hours luxuriating in the blissful calm of the spa, streaming our own happy music playlist via the hotel Wi-Fi, and were joined for a short time by only two other guests, Alan and Lydia, an English couple looking to buy an apartment in Val d'Isere. They were excellent conversation and didn't seem to mind that we were wandering around in just our pants. The last time we'd been in a spa we'd found ourselves unexpectedly in a naked sauna, not an entirely unpleasant surprise, but this time we were keeping our undies firmly at the tops of our legs.

Although they were older than us, listening to Alan and Lydia's stories of still feeling trapped in work, despite having recently sold their business for a decent amount, sounded so familiar to us, reminding us how fortunate we were to have taken the plunge into something new when we did. Whatever work we find ourselves drawn back to in the future, we hope that our experiences on the road (however long they last) guide us into projects we care about and can tackle with enthusiasm rather than the 'pushing on' mindset we used to take with us on our commute to the office. Then again, as Henry David Thoreau said, "I make myself rich by making my wants few", which is definitely something that living in a motorhome has shown us. Because we literally can't carry a lot, we have learned to live with far fewer possession around us and discovered an enormous freedom in that, plus significant clarity on how little we actually need. It also helps us to appreciate little luxuries far more when we are exposed to them.

Back in the spa at Hotel Avancher, we couldn't stop smiling. It was just so wonderful to be out of the cold and surrounded by comfort that we almost didn't want the day to end. We were a little unsettled by our complete lack of food and increasingly growling tummies, but when Esther popped downstairs in the evening to take a look at the restaurant menu, she ended up being given an armful of fruit as a gift. It was enough to calm our appetites until breakfast and we spent what was left of our evening chatting about where we might go the next morning?

We'd set off with a two week tour in mind, but having kind of completed three of the guidebook stages on our first day, and now having shaved off a further two days by taking the route we had to Val d'Isere, we suddenly had a lot of time in hand. Our intention to just stick to an itinerary had clearly gone right out of the window and there were now just two six-hour guidebook stages standing directly between us and our motorhome. But did we really want to be back in just a week?

The answer was no, of course, yet having gazed at our map in search of alternative loops on the outskirts of the

Vanoise we'd come to the conclusion that the only sensible way to extend our tour for an extra seven days was to cross into Italy and try a tour of the Gran Paradiso National Park. It was a route we knew almost nothing about, aside from a sketchy nine-day itinerary we'd found online. We didn't even have a map or any other details, just a handful of general paragraphs describing nine proposed stages. It was about as unplanned and unintended as a tour could get. It was also, therefore, very exciting.

In theory we had to collect two of our dogs in fourteen days' time, but we could probably do the nine hours of driving required in a single day if we absolutely had to. It would take us one day to cross into Italy, nine days around the Gran Paradiso (if the itinerary we'd found made sense), a day doubling-back to Val d'Isere and then two more days back to the motorhome (probably). That all added up to our remaining fourteen days, provided we didn't take any days off, get sick or stuck in Italy of course, which would be mean a proper hassle trying to get public transport back around the mountains.

It was definitely a gamble so we were going to have to sleep on it. Still, at least we had an especially lovely bed to do that sleeping in.

Vital Statistics – Day 5
Start: Refuge de la Femma
End: Hotel Avancher, Val d'Isere
Distance Hiked: 15 kilometres
Hiking Time: 4 hours
Height Gain: 560 metres
Height Loss: 1110 metres

Italy

Esther couldn't sleep in the night, so spent her time doing the fiddly work of cutting and pasting the descriptive paragraphs we'd found about a tour of the Gran Paradiso into a file on her mobile phone. This, along with the names of the start and finish locations, occasional waymarks and some estimated stage times jotted down on a sheet of hotel notepaper was to be our provisional Gran Paradiso 'map'. We didn't have a clue what the distances were, or the height gains since they weren't mentioned, just that the total walking time was estimated at fifty hours over nine days.

But we'd decided to give it a try anyway. We were excited to be doing something we'd previously never even contemplated before, not to mention a little bit nervous, but mostly we were just hungry. Not hungry for adventure I hasten to add, but hungry for food. The fruit snack we'd been given the previous evening had been generous and welcome, but our mountain-worked bodies had metabolised it in about quarter of an hour and woken us up with a loudly shouted demand for calories. Lots and lots of calories.

Our resolution to eat a sensible, healthy breakfast lasted for about three and half seconds after we arrived at the hotel buffet. A small bowl of muesli and some fresh fruit was suddenly the last thing on our minds when our empty stomachs caught sight of the opulent heaps of fresh bread, cereals, exotic fruits and, mostly, cakes arrayed before us.

I've already mentioned that we don't eat meat and prefer to eat plant-based, unprocessed foods. I've also talked in other books about our reasons for doing so as part of our cleaning up process after the challenging business years. Esther was still in her mid-twenties when a GP first suggested she start taking blood pressure medication. At the time she was about 30 kilograms heavier than she is now and I was hardly a picture of health. All of the comfort eating and binges had crept up on us, partially unnoticed as we still forced our chubby bodies to the gym whenever we had the time but also because we just didn't want to see it. I still remember the specific photo of me without a shirt on that stopped me dead, wondering who the fat guy in the picture was.

But I don't intend to bang the drum about a whole-food, plant-based diet too much here. We certainly didn't have a dogmatic attachment to it when we first tried it, just an open mind and delight at how fast the weight fell off. An awareness of how our food choices had been linked to animal suffering and environmental degradation only came later, but would ultimately become just as important as the health benefits.

Most people are more clued up about food choices nowadays, which unfortunately means a lot of supposed 'facts' float around unchecked from all sides of a debate (like most topics really). As a result, people waste time playing "you're wrong" ping-pong, digging themselves deeper and deeper into their pet perspective without any intention of ever really listening to other opinions, they're just waiting for keywords they can argue against. Trust me, I've been told more than once about the evils of avocados and how Andean villages no longer have enough quinoa to eat because "all the vegans are eating it", and sadly there is truth in that because it's the whole food system that's broken. You can justify any opinion you like by cherry-picking specific factoids, and I mean *any* opinion, on *any* topic!

Sometimes I think of the modern world as a computer full of bugs, or a house built on stilts that's massively top heavy. Layers have been added, leaks semi-repaired, holes patched over and the result, centuries later, is a confusing mix of utilities, laws, services and conflicts. Imagine if you had a blank planet and the resources to build a safe, abundant and sustainable civilisation for say eight billion people from scratch, using all of the technologies and scientific advances we have in hand today. I doubt it would look very much like the world as we know it.

But I'm digressing. The point I wanted to make is that Esther and I, after extensive research and personal experience, had made the personal choice to eat a whole-food, plant-based diet. We're not perfect, once in a while we'll give in to a slice or two of cake (though we prefer to make our own non-dairy, no-egg versions), but on the whole we just keep it simple. It just makes us feel healthier and more energised than we've ever felt before. Which is why, over the years, we've learned how to maintain our preferences when we hike and camp on the hills. It really isn't that hard, although at times we'd overdone it by hauling watermelons over mountains along with canned food and glass jars. Eventually, we'd settled on a more pragmatic approach, taking only the essential dry foods (like sensible hikers should do) and grabbing fresh food when we got the chance, at refuges and such. Or hotel breakfast buffet extravaganzas!

We started small at the Hotel Avancher, but gradually expanded until by the time we took our ninth trip to the buffet, we'd perhaps cleared away two whole cakes, in addition to several bowls of cereal and far too much toast and jam. Partly the problem was that we'd gotten way too hungry and so had compromised our usual choices. We really should have eaten a proper meal in the restaurant the evening before. But the food was also surprisingly good quality. It definitely wasn't bargain-basement, mass-produced hotel buffet food at all and we'd simply gotten greedy, something we weren't proud of and regretted very soon afterwards.

By the time we'd been in the breakfast area for an hour and a half, with countless other guests having been and gone around us, I swear I could see the waiting staff looking at us with disbelief. I mean, it's not like we're very large people but I think we'd eaten a third of our body weight.

Like a drinker who doesn't quite realise how far gone they are until they leave the pub, it wasn't until we tackled the mighty climb up two flights of stairs to our room that we got a sense of just how full we had become. My grandad always used to advise me to "stop just when you think you can manage one more mouthful". Well, that ship had sailed some time ago.

Beached on our bed, staring at our packs and the rising sun outside, we knew we had to get going if we were to make it across the border to Italy in good time, but it took a steely resolve to nip our hip straps beneath our bulging, gurgling guts and think about checking out. We knew we'd messed up by over-eating and were annoyed at ourselves for it, but it wasn't just the belly-ache that was making it hard to get going. It was also saying goodbye to such dazzling luxury so soon.

I knew it was just my usual habit emerging again, my tendency to cling on to comfort and that I should just cut the cord quickly. Still, I couldn't deny that a part wanted to take Mr Mastercard back to the reception desk and say, probably with a flourish, "another night in your fine establishment madame, and send some more of that cake to my room!"

Of course, that didn't happen. The overnight forecast of -5°C had been accurate and there was still a marked chill in the air when we stepped outside just before eleven, the official check-out deadline. Our route today would take us directly east, first along several kilometres of road to reach the Pont St-Charles, from where we would begin a thousand metres of climbing towards the Col de la Lose (2957 metres). That was the border crossing we had marked out and, from what we could make out on the edge of our Vanoise Map, would allow us to descend towards the south-western tip of the Gran Paradiso tour we'd read about.

That was the only part we could see though, just a hint of trail alongside the Colle del Nivolet. A couple of kilometres north or east and we would be relying solely on our pencilled list of names. Unless we could find a map of course, which was unlikely since nothing seemed open in Val d'Isere and there were no shops between us and the Paradiso loop.

In fact, from what we had been able to discern from the online stage descriptions, we wouldn't pass a single shop for five days until we reached the town of Cogne on the northern side of the loop. Apart from a single refuge about halfway along, all the while we were traversing the southern and eastern sides, we'd be dependent exclusively on food we could carry with us from Val d'Isere. That's why our first stop after the hotel was the only open supermarket which just so happened to be directly across the street.

It's actually quite hard to do a big shop when your belly is rebelling and telling you it "never wants to eat again, ever, not even a pea", but we managed, loading our packs with what we later added up to be more than nine kilograms of mostly dry food such as oats, polenta, couscous, dried figs, raisins, dried mango and walnuts etc., plus a little wet food like coconut cream and a few apples.

I also took the opportunity to buy some sponges, which I immediately cut into pads for the tops of our feet. Unfortunately, my big idea for "sorting out" our shoes for the remaining hiking we had planned turned out to be too little, too late. The long, wet and cold plod into Val d'Isere had caused a significant increase in the bruising, which had developed overnight into painful tenderness and swelling. Even with our laces fully undone, the slightest hint of pressure from a slice of sponge was agonising.

At first it was so bad that we did briefly consider if we could even carry on at all, but thankfully the human body is a wonderful thing and by forcing ourselves to walk along the road anyway, the pain mostly subsided into a background throb. It was a pattern that would continue for the rest of our tour, with each morning and rest stop bringing about a return of the sharpest, tendon-cracking pain and the knowledge that we just had to grit our teeth and 'walk it off'. Only on the longest, most challenging descents would it really flare up, by which time we had no choice but to keep going. Still, the moral of the story is never go walking in new shoes, not even lightweight, soft, trainer-like ones that feel great in the shop, because you're liable to suffer anyway.

As we'd left the hotel, the receptionist had implied that a free local bus service ran up and down the road outside and might take us to Pont St-Charles. Yet when we stood by the first bus stop we passed, where a digital sign told us that the next one was due in 12 minutes time, a workman came over to tell us that the bus wasn't coming. We asked if he was sure, and in answer he simply pointed towards the truck he was working with. It had a neat row of bus stop shelters lined up on the back of it, while his colleague was now busy attaching our own shelter to the sling of the truck's crane. Val d'Isere really was closed for the season it seemed. They were even taking away the bus stops.

So we walked, our poles clicking out a firm pace up to the end of the road while we waved at the handful of hardy cyclists braving a late season attempt up the Col de l'Iseran. It might have been sunny and warm on the way up but we knew from bitter experience that it was the descent that would be the killer for them. The highest cols in the Alps, those above 2500 metres such as the Col du Galibier, Col d'Agnel and the Col de l'Iseran, were ones we'd been lucky enough to cycle up more than once and they'd always been cold at the top, even in mid-August. Once, coming down the Col du Galibier, we'd had to stop several times so that Esther could thaw out her hands in my armpits, which is an excellent definition of true love I can assure you. Nice warm armpits and somebody else's frozen fingers are not a fun combination. Given the chill in the air on the morning we walked out of Val d'Isere, I had no desire at all to be cycling the remaining 12 kilometres to the top of the col.

The road walk out of Val d'Isere may have been relatively 'dull' compared to what lay ahead, but it gave us time to warm up and walk off some of our over-sized breakfast. It also gave us a chance to enjoy the promise of the fresh snow that was dusting the highest peaks. The valley immediately around us was still green but above was a world of white slopes, a world we would be entering fairly soon.

When we reached the hairpin at the Pont St-Charles the road veered right, snaking towards the Col de l'Iseran, while we continued straight on, re-entering the Vanoise National Park on a well-made path towards Refuge du Prariond (2324 metres). Rising first through a steep-sided gorge, with l'Isere river raging through the channel, the path soon entered another broad, green bowl ringed by snow-dusted 3000 metre peaks and ridgelines. Behind us, framed by the sides of the gorge, was the sharply pointed summit of La Grande Motte with La Grande Casse, the highest summit in the Vanoise National Park, poking out just to the side. That was what we were saying goodbye to, at least for a while.

We quickly made our way along the flat valley floor to reach the Refuge du Prariond, finding a half-covered shell surrounded by portacabins and an army of orange-vested workman enjoying lunch. A sign informed us that the refuge had been closed since September 2018 and would remain so until Spring 2020, at which time there would be a brand new building to welcome guests.

We'd made good time from Val d'Isere, reaching the refuge in just ninety minutes, so we elected to continue straight on. A signpost suggested it would take us another two hours to ascend the 600 metres up to the border at Col de la Lose, and after our relatively late start we hoped to get the climbing out of the way. Besides, it's not like we were even close to needing a snack yet, our bellies still wobbly with breakfast buffet.

We began rising up above the valley floor, initially on well-trodden, deep tracks in the grass but these soon began to give way to stonier trails. Sections of bare mountainside also began to creep in, with channels of water still frozen by the recent cold snap. Enormous icicles clung to overhangs while intricate and beautiful constructions of wind-blown sleet had formed on the wind-sheltered side of cairns and boulders. With an almost totally blue sky above us and a warm sun, it was a remarkable scene to be walking through, as though Jack Frost himself had danced across the hillside and left snowflake art in his wake.

By the time we were a couple of hundred metres below the col, a shallow saddle in the long ridge across the valley head, we were crunching through fresh snow ourselves, still several inches deep. With the increasingly deep layer of snow totally masking the path, we found ourselves forced to take a best-guess route to the top, especially the final stretch which kicked up steeply towards the ridge. Sliding suddenly backwards at times, our legs occasionally vanishing up to the knees in snow drifts, we struggled upwards while hoping that we were at least staying relatively close to the trail. Looking down into a black glacial lake, we could see nothing but steep, snow-covered surfaces between us and a very cold impact indeed.

When we did make it to the top it was with some relief, but mostly with exhilaration at the sudden sight of the Gran Paradiso massif hulking out of the Earth directly in front of us. Not only were we now on the border between two nations, but we were on the border between two national parks, which between them create the largest nature reserve in Western Europe. Behind us, to the west, was the grand canvas of the Vanoise, a spectacle we had spent the past six days walking through, and before us was a haven as yet unknown. The Gran Paradiso peak itself, the only 4000 metre-plus summit to sit entirely within Italy at 4061 metres, stood proudly above its neighbours, its glaciated flanks sitting amid a predominantly north-south string of smaller summits strung across the eastern horizon.

The park which bears the name of this peak was originally established in 1922, Italy's first national park, and today covers over 700 square kilometres of Alpine terrain, taking in forests and pastureland in addition to the high mountain slopes at its heart. Almost 10% of the parks surface is officially covered by glaciers and with an average altitude of 2000 metres, there is an abundance of Alpine beauty to be found within. The roots of the park go back to the mid-1800s when the soon-to-be king of Italy, Victor Emmanuel, created the hunting reserve of Gran Paradiso in response to the dwindling numbers of ibex. Hunted partly for sport but mostly because their bodies were believed to contain therapeutic powers, numbers were down to less than 100 animals at the time.

In 1920, when his grandson King Victor Emmanuel III gifted the original 21 square kilometres of park, numbers were estimated to be around 4000. Despite the park being formally established two years later, poaching pulled numbers back down into the hundreds, although today they are estimated to stand again at close to 4000.

This was the reserve that we would enter into the moment we started our descent from the Col de la Lose, which we did after just a short pause. Wielding several three-foot-long icicles like light-sabres, we stormed into Italy like chilly Jedi, or at least I did. Esther was much too sensible to make zhoom-zhoom noises and attempt a spinning kick on top of a steep scree slope (I totally nailed it though). Thankfully there was much less snow on this east-facing side of the col as we began lowering ourselves down towards a large lake, the Lago Serru, using a series of painfully-cold chains to slide backwards across the loose mountainside.

After the chains came a series of hard-packed switchbacks across dark rock to reach a grey plateau, where multiple threads of water flowed together into a single powerful stream that plunged down the next rocky step. Another series of chains, ladders and D-rings carried us down close to the waterfall, bringing us to a large yellow building identified on our map as the Plan della Ballotta, the first bivacco of our adventure so far. Prior to this summer we'd never even heard of bivaccos, but had since become aware of just how prevalent they are in Italian mountain ranges. They're basically unmanned shelters, usually fairly small although a few are as large as some refuges, and they get occupied on a first come, first served basis. The tour of the Gran Paradiso we were about to attempt had us staying at a few of them, provided there was space. Otherwise we'd have to camp outside.

Unfortunately for us, this particular bivacco was locked and could only be accessed by collecting a key from either the Refuge du Prariond back in France (the one that had been closed), or the Rifugio Citta di Chivasso over on the Colle del Nivolet, which we could just about see far in the distance. We had hoped some other people might already be there and have it unlocked, but it wasn't to be, so we had little choice but to continue descending.

We'd double-checked back in our hotel room, so we already knew that wild camping in the Gran Paradiso National Park, as within the Vanoise, is only allowed within certified campsites, a rule we had no desire to break. The rules did contain a caveat stating that for "emergency reasons Alpine bivouac for just one night is allowed if there are no shelters in the area or they are full", which we took to mean we could camp very high up if we got to any of the bivaccos and found them already occupied, or if we just couldn't make it and were on a high pass. However, that didn't mean we wanted to take advantage and deliberately plan to get ourselves into such circumstances.

From our current position, the closest formal place to stay was the Rifugio Citta di Chivasso and to reach it required us to descend a few kilometres to the S460 road and then climb again for several more kilometres, albeit gently. That would put us on the loop of the Gran Paradiso that we'd seen described and would give us a legitimate place to stay. We guessed it would take us at least a couple more hours walking though, unless we could hitchhike when we got to the road.

We reached the road an hour after the bivacco and we did manage to flag down a couple of passing cars, but neither of them wanted to take us with them up the road towards the refuge. It probably didn't help that we spoke almost no Italian beyond "buongiorno", "grazie" and "parla inglese?" The second of the cars, however, did somehow manage to convey the message that we should cross the nearby dam at the end of Lago Serru and ask at the building there. We had no idea what the building was, but there was a car parked outside of it and we reasoned that we had no better option for the time being. At the very least we could ask for permission to camp outside of their building.

Ten minutes later we rang the doorbell and were greeted by the smiling, slightly confused face of a middle-aged man. We used a "buongiorno, parla inglese?" combination, which resulted in a younger man being called from another room.

To cut a long and somewhat limited conversation short, their names were Paolo and Emilio and they were responsible for monitoring the turbines and other equipment linked to the network of dams in the area. English words did feature in the communication, but mostly we relied on smiles and arm-waving, ultimately receiving a happy blessing to camp outside of their building for the night along with an invitation to join them for some drinks and warmth if we wanted to.

Finding a nice spot overlooking the lake, we put up our tent and had our dinner just as the sun began to dip behind the ridge we had crossed a few hours earlier. Although we were camped alongside an abandoned concrete bunker, a relic of a more violent time in Europe's history, the light reflecting on the broad surface of Lago Serru created such a soft atmosphere in this idyllic hanging valley that it was hard to believe anyone had the heart to build an instrument of war up here at all.

That we were then able to enjoy the delights of an unexpected warm shower and steaming cups of tea was simply the icing on the cake. We'd only gone back to visit Paolo and Emilio to ask for some drinking water, but been ushered in and plonked down at their dining table to join them. Set to a background soundtrack of politicians arguing, waving their arms and throwing paper at each other on Italian TV, an all-too-familiar display to us that had Emilio shrugging and saying "bambini", they made their own dinners and gave us a brief overview of the intricate system of dams, tunnels and turbines they monitored during their five-day residential shift. Fortunately, they had diagrams in a manual to explain things to us and were clearly very proud of their work and role in generating electricity for their communities. But more than that, they were just incredibly nice guys. Even though we could hardly communicate, they made us feel unbelievably welcome as we sat at their kitchen table nodding and smiling at one another.

They also wanted to hear about our own adventure, showing us to a corridor with an enormous map of the entire Gran Paradiso National Park blown up on the wall. It was like a gift from the heavens for us. Here we were, right on the verge of stepping off our current map, and suddenly two guys in an engineering cabin present us with exactly what we needed. We couldn't take it with us of course, it was pinned down, but we could take as many photographs as we liked as we talked Emilio and Paolo around our planned loop.

Traced out on the map like this it suddenly looked much more real to us, while our hosts made it clear they thought we were mad. They loved the mountains, no doubt about it, but they especially loved them from their warm cabin from where they could watch the ibex and foxes in comfort. The photographs they showed us of their workplace in winter were fantastic.

As the twilight dimmed to darkness outside, we said our goodnights and made our way back to our canvas home, the short walk illuminated by the spotlights strung across the length of the dam. We couldn't believe how well we'd fallen on our feet. We'd basically blundered into Italy with minimal planning only to find ourselves warm, showered and much better informed than we had been when we set out. "Roll on the morning", we thought, "it's time to get going around the Gran Paradiso."

Vital Statistics – Day 6
Start: Hotel Avancher, Val d'Isere
End: Lago Serru
Distance Hiked: 15 kilometres
Hiking Time: 5 hours
Height Gain: 1160 metres
Height Loss: 680 metres

Invisible

The marvellous scenery surrounding Lago Serru had completely vanished by the time we woke up, replaced with a thick mist that hid even the ends of guy ropes. We'd heard a smattering of rain in the night and had been aware of low clouds during our nocturnal toilet trips, but nothing had prepared us for such a dense blanket of invisibility by the time we woke up.

With unfeeling fingers we stuffed away our sleeping gear and tent and made our way back to Paolo and Emilio, finding a warm welcome waiting on the doorstep in every sense of the word. Breakfast was a very different experience to what it might otherwise have been. Instead of huddling on a damp stone, wolfing down soggy cold oats in a hurry to get moving, we were able to cook some honey-sweetened porridge while lingering over a warm cup of tea. In the background, MTV was blasting out some sort of dance music that didn't quite fit the peaceful breakfast scene, with men wearing pink pom-poms convulsing like they'd been tasered, but it didn't matter because we couldn't understand a word of what they were rapping about.

Shortly after eight Paolo and Emilio let us know that they had to start work, but were happy to give us a lift towards the Colle del Nivolet on their way to check another turbine station if we wanted? We could have bitten their arm off. Not only would that save us up to 500 metres of uphill walking in search of the route we'd traced out, it would hopefully set us squarely on the right track. Although we hoped the mist might lift or clear a little later in the day, at the moment we could still hardly see their car from the door of the cabin.

It was a wild ride towards the col. Emilio was driving and Paolo, all six-foot-six of him, was scrunched up against the dashboard with his knees close to his ears in an attempt to give us some legroom in the back of their tiny Fiat Punto. Racing through the mist on slick roads, we went uphill like we were winning the Monaco Grand Prix, veering tightly into bends while Emilio and Paolo chatted in the arm-flailing, animated way that Italian men use when talking about anything at all.

I remember the time our motorhome broke down in Italy and we travelled with the tow truck driver to the garage. On the back of his flat-bed truck was our home containing our beloved dogs and pretty much everything else that was important to us in the world, and he was steering with his knees along a narrow country road so that he could flap his arms about while talking about football on his phone. He was about as relaxed as it is possible to be and still be awake, and I was as tense as a tuning fork watching huge trucks barrelling towards us. It was one of the longest thirty minutes of my life.

Riding with Emilio and Paulo, by comparison, was just a Sunday pootle, even with the tyre screeching and G-forces equivalent to a moon shuttle take-off. Somewhere along the way we crossed another small dam, but that was the only landmark we noticed during the six minute journey to the unremarkable corner they stopped at. This, they assured us, was the trail, a brown and muddy puddle that extended into the fog with what looked like a cow stood at the other end of it. The air was lung-tighteningly cold as we stepped out of the small car, hugging and giving profuse thanks to our unexpected hosts. And then, with a final wheelspin turn, the Punto vanished back downhill.

Taking out our camera, we studied the photographs we'd taken of the black and white map and tried to locate ourselves. Obviously, we hadn't been taken all the way to the Colle del Nivolet, because there was no sign of the refuge, so where were we? Our notes contained the following information for the stage ahead of us – "Rif. Chivasso – Alpe Comba – Punta Rocchetta – Colle della

Porta (3002 m) – Bivacco Giraudo (2630 metres). Always open. 4.5 – 5 hr". That was it, letter for letter. That was all we had to go on and we could only find a couple of those names on the photographs, no matter how much we zoomed in.

After several minutes we decided to just get walking, starting a traverse into the fog that we hoped would take us in the right direction. We passed under the outlines of pylons and alongside what looked to be a refuge of some kind, although it was closed, before finding our first reassuring marker – a wooden sign with the words A. Comba etched into it, a place that was actually in our notes. Shortly after that the path began climbing uphill, mostly sticking to broad rocky tracks that were clearly man-made. These were the mule-tracks constructed by King Victor Emmanuel II after creating his hunting reserve way back in the mid-1800s.

Between 1860 and 1900, 325 kilometres of mule-tracks were built or restored in the park, linking up five "royal hunting houses" situated at an altitude of between 2000-2200 m. The mule-tracks were organized into a main backbone of 150 kilometres that linked the royal houses, plus 175 kilometres of off-shoots towards wardens' lodges and hunting stations. The "backbone" was designed to allow quick access to the hunting houses and make the steep slopes and ravines easier to pass. Regardless of whether the royal entourage was coming from Turin or Valle d'Aosta, the tracks made it possible to easily get to any of the houses on horseback, with a constant gradient of 8-10%, wide bends and paved tops.

And that was what we were now following, making it a relatively easy and undemanding climb through the otherwise unvarying mist. Which was great, because after an hour it started snowing again, adding to the already snow-covered mule track which would have otherwise been much harder to pick out on the ground.

We knew, from our photographed map, that before crossing the 3002 metre Colle della Porta, we first had to cross the 2911 metre Colle della Terra, which we did two hours after saying goodbye to the relative safety of Emilio and Paolo's car. At no point during the day had the mist looked like lifting at all, and now at 2900 metres we were in a world defined by just a few metres of semi-snow-covered mule track. The rest was just a bubble of grey that moved with us, and if either of us got more than five metres ahead of the other, then they disappeared.

It was disconcerting, but it was also quite exciting. This really did feel like proper adventuring, close to 3000 metres, fully-layered up against the biting cold, our hoods tight around our heads and not another soul available to help us if we needed them. We were lost in the void, except we hoped we weren't actually lost.

We descended for twenty minutes after the Colle della Terra, arriving at a sign for a lake that we couldn't see (Lago Lillet, 2787 metres) and then began climbing once again on what felt like a ridge, because the limited ground we could see curved away on both sides. Several times we had to cross huge snowdrifts that completely covered the mule track, many of which we couldn't see the other side of when we started. One, it turned out, covered a bend in the track and left us floundering around in sometimes waist-high snow for five minutes trying to find the trail again. There was very little in the way of painted markers, at least that we could see, although when we did spot a pair of red-and-white stripes it was always a great relief.

By the time we crossed the Colle della Porta we'd been walking for three hours and could feel the cold starting to overcome us. A sign close to the Colle della Terra had estimated an hour to this point, which had been spot on, and 1 hour 50 minutes to the Bivacco Giraudo, so we hoped we could get out of the cold in less than hour.

The bivacco was the place that our notes suggested we stay and we certainly had no intention of trying to go any further in this foulness. Esther's hands had long since lost all feeling even though she'd kept them tucked in her armpits and now, because she hadn't been using her arms with her trekking poles, she said she could feel her whole upper body starting to shut down.

We began downhill for a second time, still following a snowdrift ridden mule track while eagerly scanning the grey for signs of a shelter of some kind. We didn't know what we were looking for, or even how big it was. Yet we didn't see anything. I was keeping an eye on my watch, since time was pretty much the only guide we had of our progress through the grey.

We did cross a rocky, watery plateau after half an hour but that seemed too soon. Yet by the time another hour had elapsed and we were re-entering grassy territory on a series of long, gradual switchbacks, I was starting to worry we'd missed it. We had no idea how much altitude we'd lost but the snow had turned to rain by now, a fact that was doing nothing to help us keep warm.

After four hours in the cold and mist, without stopping, we were beginning to doubt ourselves. Had the bivacco been up on that watery plateau? Should we double back to check? What if it's only just below us? Questions were racing through our minds and all the while we were getting colder.

We'd been getting the camera out every now and then to stare at the black-and-white photographs, but apart from the suggestion that the bivacco was close to a lake, we'd almost totally lost our bearings by now.

In desperation, I suggested Esther stay put while I left my bag to run downhill for five minutes. That way, we could find out if it was still below us, or not, and then make a resolution on whether to double back. So that's what we tried, only to further confuse matters when I did indeed discover a flat, grassy plateau with a lake on it, but no signs of a shelter no matter how much I frantically searched in the mist and now pouring rain.

My five minutes had rapidly become ten, so I stumbled back uphill in search of Esther. I was running, as best I could, and sweating hard in my waterproofs, but I just couldn't find her. I couldn't believe how far I'd run and in my tiredness I could feel a rising panic that I'd even managed to miss Esther somehow.

I was so relieved when she appeared coming towards me that I just gave her a huge, soaking wet hug. She'd gotten too cold waiting, despite doing star jumps, and was heading downhill now to try and warm herself up. I explained that I'd found a lake but no shelter, so we had another check on the camera before agreeing that doubling back was just foolish now. We'd obviously missed the shelter somehow, even though we'd been looking, so there was no guarantee we'd do any better by going uphill again. The best we could do was push on for another twenty minutes or so and if we didn't find a better option, we'd just have to pitch our tent and wait until the weather improved.

I retrieved my pack from a place where the rain was still just solid enough to settle as a slushy pile on the cover, and caught Esther up just as she reached the wet, grassy plateau. Together, we found a red-and-white marker, so we followed that, and then found another couple which at least reassured us we were still on a trail of some kind. The rain continued to hammer down, creating a thunderous rumble in our ears through our hoods.

Almost five hours after setting out, without a single rest, we eventually found a sign pointing back up a different trail towards Bivacco Giraudo. We had no clue what we'd done wrong, but since the sign suggested it was an hour away we'd evidently missed it by some margin. This left us with a decision. Standing in the rain, we could both feel exhaustion overwhelming our bodies, and I could particularly see Esther fading fast which deeply worried me, but I also believed that the bivacco would provide much more shelter than our wet tent in this foul weather.

So I made a proposal. We'd power-march uphill with all we had left in our tanks for thirty to forty minutes. It would not only warm us up, but if this sign was telling the truth then we should be able to make it to the bivacco in that time. If not, we'd pitch our tent wherever we stood, get in our sleeping bags and wait until tomorrow.

Esther agreed, so off we went. Passing wet rocks, muddy puddles and occasional orange paint marks, we felt the ground rise steeply as we veered beneath cliffs that we couldn't see the top of. On and on it went, the minutes ticking away towards our agreed "give up" time. Twenty, thirty, thirty-five…. "It's there" I shouted at one point, but I'd only mistaken the silhouette of a pointy boulder for a shelter. But I wasn't wrong the second time.

The relief and elation when the yellow-coloured, metal hut emerged from the mist was hard to describe. It looked like little more than a garishly painted garden shed with a rounded roof, but after a little over 5 and a half hours of non-stop walking, through snowdrifts and a body-numbing cold, I felt like I had just won the lottery.

We prised open the heavy door to find a haven of wood-panelling with bunk beds and a small table. Two bunks were already unfolded close to the roof, which was only a couple of metres tall as it was, while the other four were folded away like in an old-fashioned train carriage. Each was little more than a metal frame supporting a network of springs and a thin foam pad on top. A tiny window above the door let in a sliver of light, but it did little to illuminate the dark wood and there was no pretending there was any warmth awaiting us within. There was no wood-burning stove we could light, just a small wood-and-metal box at 2630 metres with four inches of snow on its roof. Still, it was even more welcome than our plush room at the Hotel Avancher had been.

We bustled in, dripping water everywhere and with shaking hands unpacked our stove to prepare a pan of hot food. Sitting on opposite benches with five blankets each wrapped around us, we waited with hunger pangs for a pan of lentil pasta to be ready and inject some warmth into our bodies. We'd also jammed a couple of blankets down the edge of the door, which didn't quite close properly and had been letting in a vicious draft.

More than anywhere else it was our feet that hurt. Our already disliked hiking shoes had been overwhelmed by the snowdrifts and despite being Gore-Tex-lined, the snow falling into them had left our feet both sodden and frozen. The numbness had blocked out the usual pain the shoes gave us, but it would be several hours and three saucepans of hot food later before we began to regain anything we could reasonably call sensation in our feet again.

Hoping that nobody else would arrive and need to share the blanket collection, we each crawled up onto a top bunk, wrapped our sleeping bags and a pile of blankets around us and slept for what remained of the afternoon, stirring only when the call of nature demanded it.

At the start of the book I alluded to my chronic health problems and some medical equipment I need to use, though I didn't go into it, partly because if you've read my other books you already know what I'm talking about but also because the more hiking adventures we take, the less of a big deal it is for me personally. That said, this day was the exception. Due to a birth defect, I have always lived with bowel incontinence, though I mostly hid it and dealt with it alone until seeking medical help in my late twenties. Nowadays, I manage when I go to the toilet using a sort of DIY enema kit that I need to use whenever my body lets me know it's time.

So far, in the Vanoise particularly, I'd always been at a refuge or other toilet when that time came, so the outdoor enemas I'd grown familiar with on other trips hadn't featured. Unfortunately, in Bivacco Giraudo, it was time to reacquaint myself. I'd have to use my kit outdoors plenty of other times during our time around Gran Paradiso, but none more challenging than the thirty-five minutes I spent with my arse out in a blizzard on this particular afternoon. Still, as payback for that thirty-five minutes I got my entire evening back, which is why I'm so grateful I did finally seek medical help for a condition that so many people suffer with in silence.

The inside of the bivacco had warmed ever so slightly with our presence during the afternoon, but it was still bloody cold by early evening when we stepped outside to discover a startling sight. After an entire day of shocking weather, the clouds had finally lifted while we'd slept to reveal just a hint of the spectacular scenery that we were surrounded by.

We couldn't see too much, but we could see the deep Valle dell'Orco beneath us and the small green hanging valley I'd been dashing around in the rain looking for this shelter. We could also make out the shelf we were sitting on, still largely snow-covered but there was a definite change in the air that suggested the snow wouldn't last the night. It was no longer as bitter and felt a little more like the normal evening chill you'd expect on such a high mountain perch. There was even a hint of pink in the sky to suggest that somewhere, possibly not too far away, the sun was trying to break through. As we said our goodnights to each other and retreated to our respective bunks, swaddled beneath sleeping bags and several blankets each, we both dearly hoped that it would by the morning. It had been fun and exciting for a day, but this sort of cold and wet wasn't an experience we wanted to endure for days on end.

"If it's like this again tomorrow, I'm getting a bus" I said to Esther as we flicked off our head torches and snuggled down.

Vital Statistics – Day 7
Start: Lago Serru
End: Bivacco Giraudo
Distance Hiked: 14 kilometres
Hiking Time: 5 ½ hours
Height Gain: 950 metres
Height Loss: 770 metres

Sunshine

We woke to the sight of a gentle purple light drifting through the tiny window above our bunks. The temperature had continued to rise steadily throughout the night, allowing us to eventually dispense with the extra blankets and spend most of the time in just our sleeping bags. When we cracked open the door we were met by a multicoloured sunrise forming the backdrop to a spectacular combination of mountain scenery.

Various ridgelines fluttered across the distant southern horizon, silhouetted by the ever-changing sky, while on the other three sides high cliffs hemmed us in. To our right was the snowy Colle del Porta that we'd crossed in the mist, while behind us the rock shot up almost vertically towards the Becca di Monciair (3544 metres) and its nearby sister peak Ciarforon (3642 m).

The small plateau the bivacco stood upon had completely cleared of snow in the night, leaving just the bright yellow of the hut itself to add some contrast to the purple-hued grey stones tossed around the grass. With those majestic cliffs behind us, it was easy to feel very small and frail in the vastness of the mountains here. It was certainly a heavenly setting to have woken up into.

Grateful for the simple existence of this marvellous shelter, we said a quiet thank you to Ettore Giraudo, the man who donated the structure to commemorate his daughter, Margherita, way back in 1950. As we re-stowed our bunks and re-folded all the blankets we'd used, we were careful to ensure everything was just as we'd found it. Who knew when the next visitors in need would arrive? A guestbook suggested it had been in regular use over summer, but for the previous week there had been nobody. We also slipped the suggested donation into the honest box on the wall.

We started down the hill shortly after nine, just after the sun arrived at the bivacco to drive away the remaining morning chill. As we set out, we were now able to clearly see precisely where we'd gone so wrong the previous day while blundering blindly in the fog. Across the now crystal-clear air we could easily make out a traverse directly from the flat, watery plateau beneath the Colle del Porta towards the bivacco. That's what we'd missed it in the fog and why we'd ended up taking so painfully long to descend and re-ascend via another route.

Oh well, it didn't matter now. Everything had turned out okay in the end, as it so often does. Our 'detailed' instructions for the day told us to look out for "Alpe Gran Piano (hunting lodge), Bocchetta del Ges (2692 metres) *Steep & Care! Biv. Ivrea (2770 metres) 9 Spaces – 5.5 – 7 hours".

If you're thinking that makes little sense, I assure you it made just as little sense to us when we wrote it. Fortunately, there'd been an A4 sheet in Bivacco Giraudo showing a more detailed map towards Bivacco Ivrea. We couldn't take it with us, naturally, but we had been able to get a better photograph to help us if the signs failed us throughout the day.

After retracing our steps downhill to the point we'd reached the previous afternoon, we followed an easy traverse eastward along a grassy hillside that slanted left-to-right sharply, plunging into the deep Valle dell'Orco far beneath us. An hour later we reached the pink-walled, single-storey hunting lodge at Alpe Gran Piano (2379 metres), one of Victor Emmanuel II royal hunting lodges a century and a half earlier. Today it serves as an unmanned refuge with 10 beds according to a sign outside, something which we may have found interesting the day before had we been better prepared for this little loop we were attempting.

After the lodge we found ourselves back on the ever-gentle mule tracks, zig-zagging up the hillside towards our first pass of the day, the Bocchetta del Ges at 2692 metres. Only near the very top did the integrity of the mule track falter, making this one of the gentlest, easiest climbs we'd enjoyed all summer.

From the top, where we enjoyed a short lunch stop, there wasn't a single sign of human influence on the landscape in any direction. All we could see on either side of the col was green hillside, crags, scree slopes, boulder fields and summits hanging on to the very last of their recent snowfall. Although the peaks were lower, in absolute terms, compared to others we had seen in the Swiss Alps, because everything was on the same scale the outlook looked larger somehow. Nothing in particular dominated the view or drew the eye, it was all just part of the same colossal scene. A beautiful void that felt so close it was like a magnificent canvas you could reach out and touch.

Starting down from the Bocchetta, we were initially worried about the terrain as we were looking down on a lot of loose rock with no clear path. However, as usual, the snaking, winding mule track found a way to weave through the tumult and deliver us safely to a marshy plain at 2400 metres. More gentle climbing followed, negotiating crags and streams beyond the plain before cutting through a shallow canyon where we surprised a herd of ibex.

With their iconic status in the park we'd expected to see some, but this herd of some 13 graceful animals clustering behind what seemed to be the stockiest, elder male was an unexpected gift. We'd read that an individual horn can weigh over six kilograms, and we could well believe it looking at the eighteen-inch-long, ribbed and fiercely pointed specimens scattered throughout the herd. Given that ibex can also weigh well in excess of 100 kilograms, I wouldn't have fancied any of them charging at us. Yet once they'd gotten over their initial shock, they didn't seem at all phased by our presence and continued to chew the cud, with just a few males keeping an eye on us as we walked silently within a few metres of them.

Another short descent, followed by a brief climb later, and we arrived at the Bivacco Ivrea (2770 metres), yet another yellow shed in a sea of remote green and grey. We'd been walking for less than 5 hours and it was still only early afternoon, so we knew we'd probably carry on a little further that day even though we'd reached the end of the suggested stage.

The weather was generally okay, despite a cold wind that was just starting to build outside and besides, we already had it in mind to complete the nine day itinerary we were using in less time, if we could. It would give us time in hand for later on, if we needed it, but it also meant pushing on when we had the chance, like we did now.

The next stage on our description said "Colle dei Becchi (2990 metres), Rif. Pontese (2217 metres), Bocchetta di Valsoera, Rif. Pocchiola Meneghello (2440 metres). 5.5 – 6 hrs".

We knew immediately that we couldn't manage all of that, either physically or before it got dark, but we hoped that if we could at least get to the middle refuge, the Pontese hut, then we'd have made a good start on chipping away at those nine days. We still took half an hour to hide in Bivacco Ivrea though, enjoying a respite from that chilly wind to eat a little snack and have a very brief lie down on one of the 9 bunks. With nobody else there, it was easy to start daydreaming of just falling asleep and not moving for the rest of the day, so it was a bit of wrench when we stirred ourselves up and began walking again.

From the bivacco we could see most of the route up towards the Colle dei Becchi. It involved a short grassy descent, a climb over a craggy rise, a traverse across a plateau and then, the hard part, a few hundred metres of climbing through a steep boulder field to reach the obvious notch in the ridgeline ahead of us. It was a high one, yes, but we were already at almost 2800 metres so we didn't expect it to be too challenging, even though a sign beneath the bivacco told us it was two hours away. "Surely it won't take us that long" we thought. We were wrong.

Following red-and-white markers, the traverse across the plateau turned out to be through a maze of boulders that we hadn't been able to see from a distance. In our flimsy little walking shoes, the tops of our feet still complaining with each downhill step, we could feel our ankles working hard to stabilise us on the uneven surfaces of the large boulders. That took about half an hour, taking us to the foot of a snow slope that led us into the main boulder chaos beneath the col.

The red-and-white markers continued here, but we soon came to the conclusion they'd been painted by an especially nimble ibex and not a human being. The physical gymnastics required to negotiate some of the leaps the markers demanded were simply beyond us, even if we hadn't been carrying a pack. And when I say 'boulders' by the way, what I really mean is that some of them were gargantuan rocks that could have crushed a bulldozer without flinching. Yes, some were 'only' the size of a family car, but others were as big as the junior school I went to, and the gaps between them were often just pitch-dark holes that I couldn't see the bottom of. To fall into one of them could well have been a one-way ticket to the big sleep. That was provided we didn't break an ankle or fracture a shin-bone on any of the razor sharp rock edges around us first. With our frequent slips and trips, our previously immaculate carbon fibre hiking poles were showing the signs of many recent scuffs and scrapes, with Esther joking that I was more worried about the poles than her.

"They're alright" she assured me, "just a few surface marks."

"Don't be silly" I replied, "it's you I'm worried about. The poles are just things that can be replaced.....but seriously though, are they okay?"

Then there was the snow to contend with. The higher we climbed, the greater the remaining snow coverage until, within a hundred vertical metres of the top, every step had to be double-checked with a hiking pole to distinguish solid rock from fragile snow-bridges. It was the sort of climb that if someone hadn't put a line on a map, you'd never believe it was actually a hiking trail. It really wasn't a very long climb but it was physically exhausting, technically demanding and seriously slow going.

By the time we did reach the top after over an hour of scrambling, scratching, slipping and sweating, we'd decided it wasn't just an ibex that had painted those markers, but a drunk ibex. Ian the inebriated ibex we called him, and unfortunately it looked like he'd been given the job of doing the other side as well. We were now stood atop a huge pile of giant-sized rubble filling the saddle of a ridge, looking out east and west at grey mountain tops surrounded by building clouds. Was the weather going to turn before dark? We didn't know, but what we did know was that we'd rather not be up in Ian's playground if it started to rain.

Thankfully, after the first fifteen minutes of jumps, hops and snow-bridge tests, we reached a long continuous snow slope that eliminated the need to cross the boulders themselves. We could simply half-ski, half-fall down a couple of hundred metres instead. A short time after that we were able to leave the boulders behind completely and join a steep but easy to follow trail down towards the Rifugio Pontese. A few low clouds had blown across the scene but nothing that had lingered for more than a few minutes, suggesting that perhaps the weather wasn't going to get too vicious after all.

As six thirty began to approach we began to accept that we'd simply run out of steam, physically and mentally. We could now even see the surprisingly shiny yellow roof of the refuge a few hundred metres below us (yellow is somewhat of a theme in the Gran Paradiso by the way), but what might have been a simple thirty minute descent earlier in the day was likely to be at least an hour at this point based on the stumbling, faltering pace we were only just managing to maintain. And then what? Arrive at half past seven and try and squeeze in some food before sleep? Both of us had needed food an hour ago, but we'd pushed on because of the need to reach the refuge.

We could still make it of course, but we both felt so unwell I made the judgement that it was foolish to keep going when we had a tent on our backs. When I'd stopped for a pee a short while earlier, Esther had fallen asleep in the sixty seconds I'd been stationary. It's incredible how quickly the fatigue can hit you at times, taking you from functional and alert to foggy-minded and crawling. From a purely physical point of view, we needed to stop.

Obviously, this meant bending the wild camping rules of the Gran Paradiso, but we supposed people would understand at 2300 metres. And, fingers crossed, they need never know since we knew we'd leave no trace behind. We'd knew we'd overdone it by pushing on from the Bivacco Ivrea and underestimating the physical demands of the Colle dei Becchi. It was our miscalculation and I didn't want to make another and one of us get hurt.

So we pitched our tent and summoned our last remaining reserves to cook a saucepan of pasta, which we devoured hungrily and chased down with some cold oats and honey. By the time we'd finished, sunset was well under way, the sky awash with a relaxing array of purples and pinks that illuminated the cliffs around us as an almost full moon began to rise in the open southern sky. In almost every other direction were spires of rock, ridges and crags, cocooning us in the arms of the mountain. And that's when it struck us. We hadn't seen any other people for almost two days now, not since Paolo and Emilio had bid us good luck. We'd expected the Gran Paradiso tour to be wild, but so far it had been as though civilisation had vanished altogether, just a few old tracks and buildings to suggest that other people had ever been here. I loved it.

Vital Statistics – Day 8
Start: Bivacco Giraudo
End: Above Rifugio Pontese
Distance Hiked: 14 kilometres
Hiking Time: 7 hours
Height Gain: 1090 metres
Height Loss: 1320 metres

An Unexpected Glacier

The almost full moon lit the night-time valley around us like an enormous chandelier, treating us to the sight of ibex silhouettes and mountain shadows when we stepped briefly out of the tent in the night. Despite the moon's brightness, plenty of stars could still be made out in the clear sky, creating an ethereal ceiling to the world in which we had made our home.

Our actual day started a little earlier than we expected when we heard a large group of hikers passing our tent at five thirty, and then another group half an hour later. We didn't know if there was something special about the trail we'd pitched alongside, but reasoning that we didn't want to be a bad example to any more hikers we decided we'd better get up and see what was going on.

Because the slope we were camping on faced southeast we got the morning sun early, and since we couldn't see any more hikers coming up the hill from the refuge we decided to use the opportunity to let our tent dry as we relaxed in the soft morning warmth. A pan of breakfast and a comfortable rock and we were in hiking heaven. We'd slept well, woken safely and were warm, well-fed and dry. All of our needs had been met.

Our list of landmarks and passes had us crossing the Bocchetta di Valsoera next, before reaching the Rifugio Pocchiola Meneghello to end the stage that we were part way through. We guessed that would take us about two to three hours of walking. Beyond that, the next stage was an eight hour monster towards another bivacco, the Bivacco Davito, that was clearly much too far to also achieve in a single day. However, there was another bivacco partway through that long stage, the Bivacco Revelli. Our notes said it was in "bad condition", whatever that meant, but even if it was totally uninhabitable we could at least justify camping outside of it, so we decided to make it our rough goal for the day.

It took us just twenty minutes to reach the Rifugio Pontese (2217 metres) with fresh legs, arriving to find a scruffy collie dog outside who wanted fuss almost as much as I wanted to give it to him. Every time I touched him he rolled on his back and began making a noise that some dog owners would call "talking", something along the lines of 'Grrern, wayow, hmmm, smee...'. Now, because of my poor Italian I can't be certain but I'm fairly sure this translates as "hello lovely human, use your paws to stroke me and I will be your friend forever". He loved it, and so did I, so much so that by the time I tore myself away from my furry friend Esther had long since vanished inside to chat with the friendly refuge guardians.

The three staff were all women, one French, one Irish and an older Italian lady called Mara who was the boss. We hadn't planned to stay very long at the refuge, but since this was our fourth day since leaving Val d'Isere we were becoming mindful of our food supplies. Potentially we might make it to the town of Cogne in just two days, but if we didn't we would probably run out of food half a day too soon. Therefore, if we could buy a few things it would help.

Mara was happy to sell us a little muesli and as many plump, juicy nectarines as we could carry. This was the only manned accommodation on this side of the Gran Paradiso loop, but it did have access to regular deliveries thanks to a winch/pulley system that ran from the end of road 350 metres further down the mountain. Yet as wonderful as those nectarines were, it was the homemade, buckwheat flour cake that most caught our eye, Mara's own creation. We started by sharing a slice, then we had a slice each and then we bought another slice just to take with us. As a present, Mara also gifted us half a loaf of fresh-baked wholemeal bread still warm from the oven.

But it wasn't just food we picked up at the refuge. They also sold maps, including one of the Gran Paradiso national park. For just ten euros we went from relying on a photograph of a photocopy and a list of names, to having our own full-colour 1:25000 impression of the park at our fingertips. Fantastic!

Before we left, Mara came over and began asking about our hike. We told her of our plans and asked if she had any suggestions for the route ahead. Our notes said that one of the passes on the long eight hour stage, the 3001 metre Colle di Motta, was "not well signed, steep and exposed".

"Don't go over Motta" she told us without hesitation. "It's a bad way. Take the Colle di Ciardoney instead. It's beautiful."

Now that we had a map, what we'd just been told was actually useful to us. Unfortunately, we didn't stop to check it out immediately, so it was only later that we realised the Colle di Ciardoney was 3152 metres high and appeared to sit at the top of a long glacial descent. However, we'd been told it was easier by a local refuge guardian and we'd always followed such advice in the past, usually finding it to be both helpful and accurate.

With a final fuss of the talking collie, who told me I was "the best human in the world", we set out to ascend the 400 metres required to reach the Bocchetta di Valsoera. Now that we had a map, everything seemed to make more sense and we felt much more reassured now that we could see how all of our route intentions fitted together.

We began the climb at quarter to ten, starting out with a series of mule track switchbacks before the path narrowed into a dirt trail. It was a very steep, craggy cliff face that we were winding our way up, alarmingly steep if we stopped to think about it, with several sheer and exposed drops that would have been non-trivial for anyone prone to wobbly legs.

At first we set a firm pace, taking advantage of the fact we were still in the shade and so allowing us to work a little harder in the cooler air. But as we reached the final, loose-surfaced push to the top, we found we had to slow down simply to avoid falling. With each step the ground seemed to slide backwards almost as far as we'd moved, leaving us grabbing on to tufts of grass and the few larger stones in search of some stability. It was here that a mother chamois and her baby appeared on a nearby ridge, the first chamois we had seen all summer. We'd seen a lot of ibex, but none of their cousins, so to see a mother and baby together was a real treat. Framed in silhouette against a background of mountains and valleys, it was such an iconic scene that we felt very lucky to have been here at just the right moment, even though we were struggling to stay upright.

Cresting the top of the Bocchetta di Valsoera (2683 metres), we found ourselves on a narrow, grassy saddle in an otherwise rocky ridgeline. Behind us was the unwelcoming sight of the scree and boulder field we'd struggled over the previous afternoon ("how the hell did we even come down that?") set within a stark grey ridge, while ahead of us lay a new panorama featuring a bright blue lake and a tangle of interweaving crags. Somewhere down there, at the unseen end of that sparkling lake, lay the Rifugio Pocchiola Meneghello and the proposed end of a stage. But we weren't going that way anymore.

The 300 metre descent to the lake shore followed an easy path across a grassy slope inlaid with moderate-sized boulders. From there we turned north, away from the lake and the refuge, heading across a plateau towards the bottom of what looked like a waterfall of stones, which is pretty much what it turned out to be. A near vertical arc of scree and debris that towered above the pancake flat plain we were stood on. Looking up, we could see a high ridge perfectly framed by the bright blue sky, a ridge with a

112

couple of small notches, any of which could have been our destination. Yet even with a map in hand, there was no way we could even begin to discern anything remotely resembling a path through the landslide in front of us. It was too steep. Too loose. Too dangerous. Surely this couldn't be the way?

But it was, and if we'd thought the few hundred metres up to the Colle dei Becchi had been tough, then what we did during the next three hours made it seem like a stroll along a quiet high street. Picking up a string of faded yellow lines painted on stones, we began climbing up the right-hand side of the scree-fall, not zig-zagging but simply walking straight up it. Sometimes we stood on large boulders while at others our feet dug into loose dust and pebbles, but the route carried on ever upwards. Occasionally the large boulders were so unsteady on their foundation that they began sliding the moment we put any weight on them. Several times I even surfed a few metres downhill on an isolated rock. It felt so precarious that we soon decided to walk at least thirty metres apart to give the follower a chance to dodge anything heavy coming down the slope.

We got a brief respite after a few hundred vertical metres, when the trail broke sideways across the scree to reach a mid-point. Here we could temporarily pause on bedrock and take a much-needed breather. It wasn't just that the climb was dangerous and physically demanding, it was also bloody hot. There wasn't a cloud in the sky and with the heat from above being reflected by the pale rocks, it felt like we were walking inside a solar oven.

There was no denying how beautiful it was though. Looking south, beyond the rubble we'd already climbed, were mountain ridges stretching away into the haze as far as we could see. We didn't know what any of it was called, but we didn't need to. We felt like daredevil explorers in this crazy, terrifying, wonderful and unique basin of stone.

113

It wasn't long after we started moving again that the temperature cooled down slightly, but only because we re-entered the world of snow that had so challenged us the evening before. We were still crossing boulders but once again were struggling to tell what was solid and what was snow? The faded yellow lines were now buried in the white and despite thinking we could make out the ghost of some footprints from a previous hiker, we didn't want to bet our lives on them. Instead, we just had to make up our own route as best we could, judging what looked safest as we moved from point to point. Occasionally, we found ourselves taking dead ends around rocks the size of our motorhome, or bigger, but as three hours of struggle approached we were excitedly stomping up the final snow-packed slope to the perfect white saddle that covered the 3152 metre Colle di Ciardoney.

We'd made it. Virgin snow stretched all around us, falling away on two sides and rising up on the other two. To our right, a sharp grey knife of rock protruded from the snow, a peak, but a peak that was less than fifty metres higher than us. We really had walked into the land of snow and summits. Behind us, looking back along that most challenging of climbs gave us a huge sense of satisfaction. We were elated, but also a little nervous when we looked ahead. It seemed we had a glacier to cross.

If you'd asked us just six weeks earlier then the answer would have been "no, we've never walked on a glacier". Since then, however, we had crossed a couple of glacial sections of trail and even rented crampons to do so on one particularly high altitude trail. But this glacier was a whole different level. It was a lot longer for a start and covered in snow, whereas the others had been exposed ice. We didn't know a lot about glaciers but we did know that snow hid scary things like crevasses. Also, we had no crampons or ice axes with us and our footwear amounted to little more than fancy trainers that hurt our feet. I'm fairly sure one of the rules about glaciers is don't cross them in trainers?

On the other hand, there was no way I was going to double back for three sodding hours after a climb like we'd just experienced. I might have done so if we'd been confronted with a twisted, contorted ice flow, but this glacier looked relatively benign insofar as we could tell. The gradient was gentle and constant so there *shouldn't* be any huge crevasses caused by the ice going over a rock shelf. Also, it was marked on our map as a hiking route, with a blue dotted line trotting straight down the middle of it which the map key told us meant "difficult foot path, mostly not marked". We did think we could see a couple of poles out on the ice, though whether we were supposed to head towards them or if they were part of some sort of glacier monitoring system we hadn't a clue.

We had a brief chat about our options and decided that we'd go slowly, one step at a time, and see how we got on. I went first, tapping my poles through the eight inches of snow onto the rock-hard glacial ice before each step. Esther followed, treading in my footsteps and fairly soon we had a good rhythm going.

After a few hundred metres of forward motion we were completely surrounded by a sea of white. White ahead. White behind. White on each side. The glacier we were on, the Glacier di Ciardoney, flows from west to east within a shallow bowl, with a sharp ridge on the southern side (our right), and a gentler, smoother ridge on the northern side (our left). Beyond the tongue, looking east, are a few more ridges and beyond those, the plains of Northern Italy.

Progress was going reassuringly well and fairly soon we grew less fearful, though we remained cautious. I was completely aware that if anything unexpected did happen to us we wouldn't be able to do a thing about it, and that it would be totally our fault for heading out onto a glacier without the right gear. If we made it, nobody would know.

But if we got into trouble I could almost imagine the scathing assessment of the situation an experienced mountaineer would arrive at.

As we lost height we began to make out long, shallow grooves in the snow covering the glacier. The grooves weren't deep, less than an inch, and we assumed they were the result of meltwater flowing over the ice beneath the snow. A couple of times we had to cross some of these grooves and our guess proved correct. The snow was more like slush at these points, forcing us to make a couple of wide detours to avoid them.

Towards the tongue of the glacier the snow was much less thick and in some places completely gone. Here we felt on firmer ground, although by now some of the meltwater channels had grown into deep and broad sluices of gushing water. Some were several metres wide, revealing a bright blue ice surface that occasionally vanished into darkness and made us feel very uneasy. That was not a place you wanted to slip into.

But we made it in one piece. Half an hour of slow-stepping and pole-tapping carried us down the glacier and back onto the unusually welcome sight of stones and scree. We immediately stopped for a pause and also to dry out our shoes in the still hot sun. Plenty of snow had found its way into our inappropriate footwear and we saw no reason not to stretch out on a warm rock and bask in the memory of what had just been some of the most challenging hiking we'd ever done. That awesomely precarious climb and then a glacier crossing! Wow, that was really something for us, and we both felt it was a special moment.

After half an hour of lounging we decided it was time to go looking for our overnight accommodation, a bivacco that was apparently in bad condition. It was only half past three so there was plenty more daylight, but we didn't want to have to rush.

It took us another hour to reach the Bivacco Revelli at 2610 metres, first crossing a dusty plateau where date markers indicated the historic reach of the glacier (another sad monument to climate change), and then following a steeper descent towards a craggy shoulder that split the valley beneath it in two. That was where the bivacco stood and, just like the others that we'd seen in the Gran Paradiso National Park so far, this one was also a small yellow shed with a rounded roof.

From the outside we couldn't see anything that suggested "bad condition", but it was only when we peeled back the three-part door that we discovered the description was totally wrong. It was like a cosy, wood-panelled country-cottage inside. Floral bed sheets covered the foam mattresses suspended on metal hammocks, the two middle bunks already set up either side of the narrow aisle, with a possible two more above and we supposed space for people to sleep on the floor as well. It was billed as a six-berth, apparently, but it would be a nightmare for six fully grown adults. It would turn the bunks into coffins and I had no idea where any bags might go. Not that it really mattered since it was just the two of us here! Evidently, since the website we'd found had been written, the interior had been spruced up and we were about to have a dream come true.

What followed was a spellbinding evening to round off a monumental day. Taking advantage of the late afternoon sun, I got naked in a nearby pool of water to rinse myself and my clothes off a little, while Esther did some stretching. Then we sat together, leaning against the warm walls of the bivacco to watch the sun dip towards the mountains we had just crossed. In the distance, looking east, we could just about make out the hazy plains of Northern Italy, while to our right was a frightening chaos of snow, boulders and scree that we would have had to descend if we'd ignored Mara and crossed the Colle di Motta anyway. No doubt there would have been a route, but we couldn't see it and it looked atrocious. We were very glad we'd taken Mara's advice.

Also, while we were sitting, we saw two rock falls break off and crash into the hillside beneath the col. Whether they were car-sized, house-sized or even larger, it was hard to tell from where we sat, but they made a huge amount of unsettling, thunder-like noise once the sound waves reached us. It was strange to watch the rocks fall in silence and then hear the destruction afterwards. It was also a reminder that while mountains fall on a geologically slow timescale overall, they can do so in a series of violent and unpredictable events and should be given respect.

Once the sun left us we retreated into the bivacco, which had built up a good deal of warmth during the day, and cooked up a simple dinner of lentils with curry spices followed by a top-up of polenta and honey. Then it was back outside to enjoy what was possibly the most satisfying sunset of our entire summer. The full moon rose through the orange haze on the eastern horizon, expanding and brightening as it gained height above the plains and entered the purple sky above us, a sky which seemed to be fading to a deeper shade every time we blinked. Gradually, the very brightest stars began to twinkle at us while the whole expansive scene seemed to soften and blur around the edges. Peacefulness was washing over the earth, bringing with it tranquillity and a clear mind. We were mere ants in this giant land, but happy ants that had been blessed with the chance to sleep in this perfect little hut so far away from civilisation.

Eventually, we submitted to the night and slipped into our bunks, but we left the door open a while longer so that we could continue staring into the face of the full moon. The hut couldn't have been better oriented to capture the scene, which is how we ultimately drifted off to sleep, with the door open and the stars arrayed above us.

Vital Statistics – Day 9
Start: Above Rifugio Pontese
End: Bivacco Revelli
Distance Hiked: 12 kilometres
Hiking Time: 7 hours
Height Gain: 1240 metres
Height Loss: 1030 metres

Civilisation

The sun rose in the channel carved by the moon. We watched its progress directly from our bunks the next morning, bursting over the ridges on the horizon like only a two octillion-ton sphere of burning plasma can. Cuddled together on Esther's bunk, we stared in silence as the ribbons of light from that initial chink grew, brightening and filling our little wooden hut with the golden light of the new day.

We ate breakfast sat on our temporary porch, savouring the calm warmth of the morning sun. This day could potentially be the final day of our loop around the isolated southern side of the Gran Paradiso tour. We'd done four very full days since leaving Val d'Isere. Today would be the fifth, and in all that time we'd seen less than a dozen people. At the same time we'd crossed passes that were wilder and felt more remote than anything we'd ever crossed before. Admittedly we'd been higher and further, at times, but this continuous stretch of near total seclusion had been unique for us. The idea of being back in a town by the end of the day was actually quite sad, especially while sitting on a sun-warmed stone atop a huge crag, directly outside of our own little country-cottage haven.

On the other hand, there was no guarantee we'd get that far. There were still two major climbs stood in our way and a very long valley descent that would probably take us at least seven hours of hiking. Also, it hadn't escaped our notice that every time the trails on our Gran Paradiso map turned to closely-spaced small red dots, it meant we were in for a tiring time of it, usually battling through a field of enormous boulders. There were several such sections waiting for us on the route ahead, so this was going to be a non-trivial hike whichever way we looked at it. At least we had just about enough food for an extra night of camping, if absolutely necessary.

Our descent from the bivacco was straightforward, weaving our way across rough ground and passing a handful of shimmering small lakes to reach the flat, green plain of the Pian della Valletta at around 2400 metres. We could now see our next target more clearly, the Colle Valletta o Finestra at 2645 metres, a broad dip in the ridge just a few hundred metres above us on the left. What we didn't expect was that we'd have so much trouble finding our way up to it.

Usually, trail markers are positioned so as to be visible in both directions, or if that's not possible then they come in pairs, one either side of a rock. Across this particular plain, however, whoever had been in charge of the paintbrush had opted for a single set of markers mostly daubed right on top of flat rocks. That would be perfect if you were navigating a helicopter, but with the morning sun almost full in our faces and turning those rocks into shiny black mirrors, it took us several false starts before we could even find our way to the bottom of the climb.

The signage problem persisted as we negotiated the initial short boulder field. Every time we looked down we could see markers stretching away nicely towards the plain, but looking up all we could see was a tangle of rubble. Normally even that wouldn't have been a problem, but the hillside between us and the top was a 75% slope of mostly grass and mud. The last thing we wanted was to lose what little trail existed to take us up there.

We needn't have worried though, since it turned out there wasn't a trail at all. A dozen or so red and white splashes scattered randomly on occasional stones suggested that somebody had been sent up here to mark the route, but evidently they'd decided not to try very hard. We came to the conclusion that it was a couple of Italian decorators who wanted to knock off early for the day.

As a result, it was proving to be yet another very precarious ascent. The grass, still damp with morning dew, was slippery enough, but it was the soft mud and pebbles that were proving harder. Every time we placed a foot it skidded instantly, forcing us to try and kick footholds into the wet earth to gain any purchase while using our trekking poles like a climber uses an ice axe. By the time we reached the top it felt like we'd just done an hour-long circuit session at the gym. It wasn't even 10 o'clock.

When we arrived, we found ourselves on the thin partition between two valleys, the Vallon della Muanda behind us and the Vallon di Lavina ahead. Back up at the head of the Vallon della Muanda we could trace out our incredible route along the Glacier di Ciardoney, while ahead of us it looked like yet another 'unpassable' anarchy of boulders. The head of the Vallon di Lavina didn't look as steep as some of the other passes we'd scaled, but we couldn't see anything that looked like a sensible route up it. No doubt there'd be a way though. There always was.

A couple of fixed ropes and a vertical ladder made out of D-rings hammered into stone were required to get down from the narrow col, before joining a series of switchbacks which carried us into the first boulder field sweeping around towards the valley head. Below us we could now see the unmistakable yellow structure of the Bivacco Davito that we knew we were basically heading towards, but it proved to be a much more challenging traverse than we had anticipated.

Up, down, jump, sidestep, big step, big step, bum slide down.....there wasn't a single moment where we were able to just relax and walk. Every inch forward required us to be completely focused on our footing, with frequent pauses to try and find the next marker or to work out the best way to negotiate the next obstacle. It was draining, both mentally and physically, and because we knew we still wanted to go a very long way before dark, it was also a little frustrating.

Which isn't to detract from the beauty of the valley, of course. We still noticed how lovely the scenery was. In many ways it was the archetypal Alpine valley, with a broad sweep of vertical cliffs standing above a wide arc of debris that narrowed as the valley sides steepened and funnelled the various water channels into a single river, thundering through the tree-lined lower slopes. In the bright sun the colours all seemed pale and washed out, grey at the top and green at the bottom, with a long, slow transition between the two extremes made up of crags and glacial detritus that slowly gave way to plant-life.

It took over an hour of struggle to reach the low point of our route, close to the bivacco, and another good hour after that to ascend to our high point for the day on the Col di Bardoney at 2833 metres. Thankfully, the higher-level signage had been much easier to follow and had directed us up to this six-foot wide, rectangular cut in the ridgeline without any major confusion. We were now stood on the boundary between two Italian regions, Piedmont to the south and Aosta to the north, the direction we were going in. Not that the regional border made the least bit of difference to the terrain but we did notice an abrupt change in sign styles, with the more familiar yellow plastic signs pointing the way down into the valley ahead of us. These were the same signs that we'd grown used to during the Italian portion of our Matterhorn tour.

We'd been walking solidly for four hours by now, so we paused for a small nibble on our remaining dried fruit. A sign informed us that we were 'only' three hours from Lillaz, the closest village some 1200 metres below us and beyond the end of the long Vallone di Bardoney. Between here and there was a long and mostly green flat-bottomed valley that looked like quite easy walking once we could get down to it.

123

Initially the trail from the col was excellent, appearing to be both man-made and well-marked with regular yellow paint splashes appearing alongside the flat-topped stones. Yet after just five minutes all of that ended abruptly, leaving us stood looking down at yet another precipitous slope that suggested just one thing, a landslide. Where there might once have been closely packed boulders was now a tumble of dust, pebbles, stones and gulleys surrounding a handful of gigantic rocks that had perhaps either resisted, or started, the fall. It looked loose and unstable and was definitely not something we could easily negotiate.

Our initial thought was that maybe we'd missed a marker or that the trail must have been re-routed, but after much staring and doubling-back more than once, we came to the conclusion that we'd have to work this one out for ourselves. Several hundred metres beneath us, where the boulders looked less disturbed, we thought we could possibly see a yellow line, but we weren't sure.

What followed was a new level for us in terms of fear. We began by taking a direction that initially climbed higher through the rubble, trying to make use of areas that didn't look as disturbed by the landslide. I don't think I've ever stood on surfaces that felt so unsteady. We were looking down at hundreds of metres of loose rubble, with more above us that felt like it was just waiting to lunge downhill. We were both trying not to think about it, focusing on one step at a time and trying not to kickstart any more slides as we tentatively chose our footing.

Mercifully, it held together, and perhaps quarter of an hour later we felt we'd traversed the worst of the landslide. We then began edging diagonally towards the yellow smudge we thought we could see, eventually stepping back onto something that resembled a narrow trail among the boulders and breathing a big sigh of relief. But even though we had found 'the path', the route remained loose and unstable. There were indeed a few yellow markers, but they kept vanishing and were mingled with some orange paint marks that suggested it was all a bit of muddle. In the end we gave up on trying to follow a trail and just made up our own program, eventually and with much relief stepping onto a mule track a good hour after leaving the top.

A few days earlier I'd occasionally been frustrated by the gradual nature of the mule tracks. There had been so many times when we could have easily taken a more direct route instead of following the 8-10% slow switchbacks. "What an inefficient route" I'd thought. Yet right now I never wanted to step back into a boulder field ever again and would have happily walked mule tracks all the way back to our motorhome.

The route from now on was easy, heading towards the end of the long Vallone di Bardoney where we skirted past a small farm and then veered left into the adjoining Vallon di Urtier towards Lillaz. We were getting on for six hours of hiking time by now, much quicker than the estimated times in our notes but still a tiring chunk of walking with only a handful of short rests. On the one hand we were soldiering on to Lillaz, but on the other it was only mid-afternoon and the sense of being on a forced march was starting to suck the fun out of it. So we stopped for an hour to doze and weigh up our options.

Today was our tenth day of hiking without a rest and the previous five days since Val d'Isere had been especially hard. All those boulder fields, painful feet and the day in the snow to Bivacco Giraudo had worn us down. The upside was that we were undeniably making excellent progress. We'd done five of the biggest Gran Paradiso stages in just four days, and with the remaining four stages being mostly shorter, we were well on track to get around the loop in just a week! That would give us at least one, possibly two days in hand. We could even take a rest day if we wanted to, but was it really what we wanted?

On reflection we decided we weren't quite ready for a rest day. Maybe we'd take one later on, we thought, but for now perhaps we should just look at getting a room for the night? That was my preferred option, to get to Lillaz and see what was on offer. Esther said she was happy for me to make the decision, which is probably why I had an extra spring in my step when we set off for the final hour or so into the busier world that awaited us.

The remaining run into Lillaz took us downhill on mostly forested tracks, where the unfortunate signs of our return to busier areas were all too apparent on the trail. After five days of near total seclusion we'd already waved buongiorno to a handful of hikers since exiting the boulder field, but it was the litter that really hammered home our proximity to civilisation. We'd seen practically no evidence of humans on the landscape for days and now, all of a sudden, were plastic wrappers, foil packets and most irritating of all, toilet paper.

I'm going to have a little moan now, so apologies in advance. Depending on which website you read, toilet paper can take anything from a few months to a few years to decompose. Yet because we all get so used to seeing it apparently disintegrate and then vanish in the toilet bowl, apparently vast numbers of people seem to think it is little more than a flimsy waft of nothing that will disappear the moment it rains a bit. And I say apparently vast numbers, because toilet paper abounds in the mountains. I can't tell you how many rocks we've gone to sit on over the years and seen shitty toilet paper jammed into the cracks. Or gone behind a boulder to find a veritable sea of turd piles and paper.

I mean, I know we all get caught short (and I'm bowel incontinent so I know what I'm talking about on this one), but why can't people just bury their shit and take the paper with them. Have we all become so germ-phobic that the thought of putting a little bit of soiled tissue into a bag to take home at the end of the day freaks us out? Or perhaps people think that just because somewhere is new and remote *to them*, that nobody else will ever go there?

Now, I make no claim to perfection on this one. The nature of my enemas sometimes makes it literally impossible to bury everything and take all the paper with me, but we do our best and I always make sure to go well away from the main trail, usually several hundred metres at least. Which is why, as we descended into Lillaz, I found myself getting irate at the unbelievable frequency of used toilet paper on the trail, or worse still – wet wipes! Most wet wipes aren't even biodegradable and can hang around for hundreds of years. Other people had gone the whole hog and had, quite literally, done a shit in full view on the edge of the path and then laid a wet wipe across it like a modern art installation.

I suppose what baffles me the most is that the people littering (and shitting on display) in the mountains are mostly people who have taken the trouble to come and appreciate nature. So why leave it degraded? Why diminish the experience for others? I don't want to sound too sanctimonious here, because I know a lot of other people do this as well, but we actually pick up litter when we see it. Every time we get to near to a bin we offload all manner of rubbish, often recyclable rubbish, that we've found on the hills. I'm definitely no environmental beacon. We all collude and use the same system one way or another, but I've never accepted the argument that "I didn't drop it, so why should I pick it up?" Okay, moan over, I think. Thank you for bearing with me.

Lillaz turned out to be a pleasant looking village a couple of hundred metres outside of the Gran Paradiso National Park boundary. There were actually two campsites still open when we arrived, but when a quick search on

Booking.com revealed a good selection of rooms in the next village on our route, Cogne, I immediately ruled out camping. Plenty of rooms were in the 60-70 euro bracket I was comfortable with and walking the extra hour to Cogne would also put us in a better position for the next day. We were tired, our feet made that fact impossible to ignore, but with promise of a room on hand it was enough motivation to keep going.

The walk into Cogne was flat and easy, mostly along a river that marked the edge of the national park. Unlike the Vanoise where we'd been constantly flitting in and out of the boundary, this little section was the only time on our entire loop of Gran Paradiso that we weren't actually *in* the national park. Arriving into Cogne we marched into busy streets that suggested summer on this side of the mountains was still going strong. Val d'Isere had been a ghost town, Cogne was a party town with every shop still open and all the restaurants doing a good trade. Situated at the confluence of four different valleys, Cogne is a popular tourist destination for both winter and summer activity enthusiasts.

We made a brief stop at the first grocers we passed to buy an armful of delicious fresh figs, which we ate as we made our way to the room we'd booked. It was our first fresh food since the nectarines at Rifugio Pontese and they were perfectly ripe, making them possibly the tastiest food we'd ever had in that moment.

The room we'd chosen, based only price and because of decent reviews, turned out to be none other than a former royal residence. The Residence Chateau Royal is a listed national monument with a tower dating back to the 11th century and was once the home residence of King Vittorio Emanuele II when hunting in his old hunting reserve. Also, it wasn't just a room but an apartment with a full open plan kitchen/dining room in addition to the bedroom and bathroom. There was even a small spa with a jacuzzi and sauna that we could use downstairs. Not bad for 62 euros! The outside was plain and imposing, a five-storey box with walls several feet thick that looked more like a mediaeval fortified tower than the name 'Chateau' might imply, but inside it was clean, simple and modern.

An especially nice touch was that because we were arriving after the reception had closed, we simply got a given the door access code and location of the key on the phone when we made the booking. We hadn't entered our credit card or passport details into any system, we were just trusted to stay the night and pay in the morning. We liked that. I know I've said it in other books but it bears repeating, trust inspires trust while suspicion breeds suspicion.

The meal we cooked that evening was nothing like our usual hiking fare. Making use of the array of pots and pans unexpectedly at our disposal, we prepared a feast of vegetables, mushrooms, beans and pasta that far exceeded our culinary requirements but left us feeling very civilised and happy after a brief visit to the little spa downstairs. It may have been a culture shock to arrive into such a busy environment after five days of only each other, ibex and marmots for company, but sealed in our private apartment we still had each other plus healthy full bellies. Our hiking clothes were drip drying in the shower. The bed was soft and the moon was shining brightly through our bedroom window. In the distance we could even hear an owl hooting. Our country-cottage bivacco had been perfect for us, yet so was this, just in a different way.

Vital Statistics – Day 10
Start: Bivacco Revelli
End: Residence Chateau Royal, Cogne
Distance Hiked: 18 kilometres
Hiking Time: 7 hours
Height Gain: 700 metres
Height Loss: 1760 metres

Up

A long way up, that's the best way to describe our eleventh day of hiking after leaving Cogne. Almost 1800 vertical metres in fact. Descending into Cogne was the first time we'd come below 2000 metres altitude since climbing out of Val d'Isere and we were soon going to be back above that threshold. Quite significantly above it since we planned to cross the 3296 metre Col Lauson before the end of the day.

We'd opted to forego a hotel breakfast this time around, electing instead to use our temporary kitchen to prepare a less crippling feast of our own before loading up our bags. In terms of extra food, we needed to have enough supplies with us to make it back to Val d'Isere, which we hoped we'd achieve within four days. That would mean shaving another day from the itinerary we'd been using, but three of the four remaining stages were short and we were confident we could do it. We'd bought most of our supplies the evening before, but while I was getting myself ready Esther sensibly went back to the supermarket for a few final extra packs of dried fruit and nuts, just in case. It meant we'd added another eight and a half kilograms to our packs, but it would be worth it.

We were ready just after nine, pausing only once on the already busy streets of Cogne to buy Esther a new hat. Somehow, I'd managed to lose mine three days earlier, which was frustrating. Not so much because of the loss of the hat but more because it went against the grain to think I'd left 'litter' of my own on the trail. Since then I'd been using Esther's hat on account of her having a lot more hair than I do, and I liked it, so she was going to get the new one. We were eager to get cracking and so bought the very first hat that fitted in the very first shop we tried. It took about forty-five seconds overall. That's my kind of clothes shopping.

Our route out of Cogne took us south-west, passing the huge green meadows known as the Prato di Saint'Orso (which are protected from any form of development) where a nearby hotel had sculpted an ornate garden entirely made up of edible plants such as leeks and lettuce. We were tracking the road towards the village of Valnontey and the weather was, once again, sunny and clear, holding the promise of another fine hot day ahead of us.

It took just forty minutes to reach Valnontey, crossing back into the Gran Paradiso National Park along the way. During the short, flat walk we'd spotted the first (and only) sign of our entire tour that bore the words "Tour Du Gran Paradis". With so many dangerous and challenging sections, and no mention on any other signs so far, we'd begun to think the 'tour' we'd set out on existed only in the minds of a handful of tourist office website managers. But now, at least, we'd seen a laminated sheet of A4 paper pinned to a fence that said otherwise.

After Valnontey our route began to steer more directly west, turning right away from the main Valnontey valley and climbing into the adjoining Vallone del Lauson. However, from the moment the climbing began it was the view towards the head of the Valnontey valley which immediately caught our eye. An immense cup of rock and ice reaching up to well over 3500 metres was framed in a huge 'V' by the greener, tree-lined slopes around us.

Our first destination was the Rifugio Vittorio Sella at 2588 metres, another of King Vittoria Emmanuel's hunting lodges. The path was broad, well-made and busy with hikers, this being a sunny Saturday in September. There was a veritable stream of multicoloured packs and dusty boots trekking upwards, at times forming what looked like the world's longest conga line.

Despite the fact that our packs were as heavily laden as they'd been all tour, thanks to the supplies we'd taken on board in Cogne, as we began negotiating the opening switchbacks I found myself power-marching like a cadet trying to pass SAS selection. In hindsight, I think my pace was due to apprehension and nervous energy coming from the knowledge that we were about to haul ourselves up almost two vertical kilometres. At the time, however, all I knew was that now I'd started, it was easier to keep going. Behind me, Esther hung on like a jogger taped to a treadmill. She knew what I was like. My 'forty-five minute specials' had become a standing joke between us over the years, characterising countless hikes and bike rides with my opening fast pace that turned me into a sweating, gibbering mess. It's why Esther usually gets to the top before me and why I've finished every half marathon I've ever tried looking like my face has melted.

As the trees grew more sparse and gave way to open mountainside, the view towards the snow-capped peaks on the opposite side of the Valnontey valley continued to inspire. The higher we climbed, the more the glaciers slipped into view to emphasise our height gain, which, mixed with the endorphins of the physical effort, created a marvellous sense of elation as we moved ever closer to that world of ice.

Nine hundred vertical metres carrying 'full food' in just under two hours was a surprising pace for us, but as the refuge suddenly materialised over a small rise in the trail, it appeared we'd done exactly that. Situated close to the mouth of the upper 'hanging valley' portion of the Vallon di Lauson, it was an undeniably idyllic spot to place a building. Green grass and sheep dominated the hillside around the lodge itself, but looking further afield every direction seemed to offer a classic Alpine view, taking in everything from snowy peaks to glaciers and crags.

The terrace outside was already bursting with satisfied looking hikers and we had no need to go in, so we simply settled on the grass a hundred metres away to nibble the grapes and juicy apples we'd bought up with us. According to the refuge website, it was a week of hunting with his brother, the Duke of Genoa, in this very area that first inspired Victor Emmanuel's hunting passion. Today, the two buildings he constructed here can host over 150 visitors who want to spend the night.

The climb beyond the refuge proved much quieter than before. Now that we'd crossed into the upper reaches of the Vallon di Lauson it was bare scree slopes and red-tinted cliff faces that dominated the scene. Passing through a herd of totally unphased sheep and a handful of bleating goats, some of whom we had to step over while they looked up at us with disinterested eyes, we climbed a gentle grassy bank before arriving at a desolate, stony plateau close to 2900 metres. This was where the final climb began, a wholly rocky and completely exposed series of switchbacks up to the equally rocky and exposed Col Lauson at 3296 metres.

After the continuous stream of people far below, we could now see less than a dozen hikers strung out along the climb to the top, making the large dry bowl around us seem just that little bit more inhospitable and remote as we kicked up the dust on the path. Although it was hard work and high, most of the path was solid and secure. There were a few tricky bits close to the col itself, narrow ledges over steep drops, with a thin blue rope fixed into the mountain to provide a little extra reassurance. But each ledge was only a few metres long and on the whole we thought this was a relatively straightforward climb to such a huge height. It's not every day you can hike to within a whisker of 3300 metres and still call it walking the whole way.

The view from the col was predictably stupendous. Like most of the others we'd crossed in the park, it was quite a small col, narrow and sharp, with thin ridges climbing away on either side to separate the respective valleys. Behind us, the upper slopes of the Vallon del Lauson flowed away from us in a pale curve, reaching towards the cloud-topped summits to the east and the vast bulk of the Monta Rosa massif in the north, its highest summits pushing right through the fluffy white clouds. Ahead of us a very different type of valley could be seen. A much more severe and rocky prospect facing towards a sea of ridges that were half lost in a haze, with just the hint of several peaks we thought we could identify back in the Vanoise National Park.

We went on to spend an hour at the col, eating lunch, having a short doze on the sun-warmed rocks and trying to discourage an especially pushy wasp who wanted to get at our honey-coated rice puffs (which were amusingly called 'Dinkelpops'). Every time we thought the little sod had gone he reappeared, stinging Esther twice on her fingers before we eventually sealed him (temporarily) inside the pot he craved so much. It seemed to be the only mutually beneficial way to stop him attacking us. He didn't seem to mind, setting about the sugary treats with no regard for the fact he was locked in with them.

Another couple arrived for a short-time but left after just ten minutes. The young lady looked very wobbly on her legs as she shakily lowered herself from the side of the col she'd sat on, reminding us how far we, and especially Esther, had come over the years.

A decade earlier we wouldn't have even contemplated a hike like this together. I still remember helping Esther down from Stickle Tarn beneath the Langdale Pikes in the Lake District, a popular route with a staircase-like gentle climb, but when the vertigo had taken over she'd hardly been able to move. Now she was sat on a 3300 metre col looking down into a tangle of rubble with a big smile on her face. It had been an incremental change, though one that had accelerated significantly thanks to the challenges of our Matterhorn tour and our recent exploits across boulder fields and landslides. Considering what we were going to encounter tomorrow, it was fortunate that we'd both developed such a head for heights.

Once our food had settled and we'd released our aggressive prisoner, we started down into the rubble, immediately passing a trio of mountain bikers who were shoulder-carrying their bikes right to the very top of the col. It's a sight we see often in the mountains, but since we don't mountain bike it's not something we closely relate to. I suppose the thrill of the descent must be worth effort though it's always struck me as a soul-breaking long struggle for a momentary exhilaration. Then again, I once went mountain hiking for a weekend with one of my brothers and he went home after the first day saying "once you've seen one, you've seen them all". As far as I know, he hasn't been back. We all like different things.

The path into the valley snaked around to create a surprisingly gentle descent into this chaotic valley head. On our right the intricate crags of the Gorgie della Grivola ridge stretched up above us, while ahead and to the left the valley was much more open. That was the direction we were taking, not all the way down into the larger Valsavarenche valley which cut north-to-south ahead of us, but in search of a smaller track that would carry us back up towards another high ridge crossing, the Colle Gran Neyron at 3295 metres.

Whether or not we'd actually do this crossing was a question we'd pondered several times since leaving Cogne. Our notes from the online itinerary suggested we should cross it, but our map had the unsettling words "via ferrata" printed alongside the little red dots which marked out the trail. In the mountains, as we'd always understood it, via ferrata has a very specific meaning. It indicates a protected climbing route, usually with a steel cable fixed at regular intervals to the mountain that allows people wearing safety harnesses to secure themselves as they climb, often using metal ladders, rope bridges and other aids along the way. They vary in difficulty, but in theory you don't need to be a climber to try them, you just need the safety kit. In the same way that we'd toured the mountains in search of cycling climbs, during our wanderings we'd occasionally met people who travelled between different via ferrata.

Anyhow, that's what we were walking towards, and if it did turn out to be a bona fide via ferrata then we had a big problem because we definitely didn't have the kit. It wasn't something we'd even tried before, and at over 3000 metres we didn't want to be taking stupid risks for the sake of a few notes pencilled on a scrap of hotel paper.

It was obvious from our map that we could simply hike down into the main Valsavarenche valley instead, and then follow the road south to rejoin the tour a little later on. We'd have missed out the high col in question and a traverse on the western flanks of the Gran Paradiso itself, but we'd undoubtedly be much safer.

We still hadn't made our decision by the time we arrived at the trail split, but started climbing towards the undecided col nonetheless. As we walked we reasoned that we might as well try the climb but under the promise to ourselves that we'd turn back, no matter how high we'd gone, if we discovered something we weren't comfortable with. In a way, I suppose it's a rule that always applies, except this time we were fairly sure we'd be turning back.

The only problem now was the question of where we'd sleep. It was getting on for early evening and, after our long sit at the Col Lauson, we obviously couldn't attempt such a crossing in the approaching twilight. We didn't really want to bend the park rules again, but since we were already well over 2500 metres we hoped that this would count as an Alpine bivouac for a couple of hikers who'd run out of daylight.

Our intention was to pitch our tent at twilight behind a long, low cow-shed that was marked on our map at 2648 metres. The shed didn't look like it had been used for some time and we did briefly consider camping inside the shed ourselves, to make sure we were completely invisible to other hikers, but decided that at this time of the day we were unlikely to encounter any way up here.

It was a worry, therefore, as we were eating our dinner to see three young men poking their heads around the corner of the cow shed to look at us. At first, we thought they might be something to do with the little radio mast we could see coming out of a metal box nearby, some sort of scientific monitoring equipment we supposed. And then, when we didn't see them for half an hour, we thought they'd maybe gone back down. But then they reappeared and we realised they weren't going anywhere. Concerned that they might be park rangers waiting to see if we were camping, we decided to bite the bullet and simply say hello. Naturally, I insisted Esther be the one to say hello. It's a tactic I usually use when I'm convinced there's no real danger, reasoning that she's far more friendly than I am. Esther doesn't always agree, but I'm certain that people (especially men) are just nicer and more tolerant when a woman asks a favour.

It turned out I was spot on about sending Esther as they were three young Belgians on a week-long camping trip themselves. By the time I wandered over everyone was happily chatting away in Dutch. Impressively, they'd simply hopped on a bus from Ghent to Geneva, caught a couple more local buses and set off with only the vaguest plan in mind. In a way, they reminded us of ourselves when we'd Interrailed as students. Back then our planning had involved booking a flight to Salzburg and tearing pages out of travel brochures on our way to the airport. It was one of the greatest adventures we'd ever had.

We spent a pleasant half an hour comparing routes and chatting with the Belgians. Helpfully, they also showed us their map which didn't use the phrase 'via ferrata' for the section above us but instead described it as 'fixed ropes'. Quite possibly it meant the same thing, but it was at least a little bit more encouraging than our own map.

We did have a little scare when I got severe stomach cramps shortly after putting up our tent. A side effect of my various bowel surgeries is that I seem to have been left prone to such pains and occasional bowel obstruction. This is a potentially life-threatening condition that is also incredibly painful, causing vomiting and obstipation and which can, in some cases, require surgery to resolve. I've been told the likely cause is 'sticky patches' (not the technical term) on my intestines left as a result of the various surgeries I've had.

Over the years I've learned to recognise the early warning signs and usually it resolves on its own, whether after three hours or thirty. More than once I have had to go to hospital as a result, but thankfully drugs and other interventions (of varying pleasantness) managed to get it sorted before surgery was needed. Either way, it hurts terribly and was the last thing I wanted in a tent at over 2500 metres.

If you've read *Just Around The Matterhorn*, then you'll know that when I feel poorly I just want to crawl into my cave and be left alone. Esther's instinct is to look after me, but we've learned over the years how best to support each other at times like this. Unfortunately, they don't usually involve being pressed together in a tent on a high mountain.

Still, Esther is wonderful and did her best to give me space, sitting outside to enjoy the starlight while I lay in my bag and tried to focus on my breathing as the waves of cramping swept over me. Fighting the urge to panic at the memory of days spent in agony in the past (I once waited 48 hours before going to hospital), I tried to lay still and just breathe, slowly in, slowly out.

I continued to breathe when Esther slipped as quietly as she could into her bag next to me, squeezing my shoulder but understanding the last thing I needed was chit-chat. And so the night dragged on.

The pain subsided at around 3 a.m. after six hours of breathing and I was so relieved I could have cried. It was a stark reminder not to take anything for granted. For the past eleven days I'd been a fit, vibrant, athletic young man, arguably in the prime of life. And then, with no warning, a tidal wave of pain had turned me into a fragile, frightened ball of agony.

But whether it's this (in my case), an accident or an unseen, unanticipated world event, the things we value the most, yet forget to appreciate, can always be taken away from us. It's why every moment is so precious.

Vital Statistics – Day 11
Start: Residence Chateau Royal, Cogne
End: Below Colle Gran Neyron
Distance Hiked: 18 kilometres
Hiking Time: 6 hours
Height Gain: 1850 metres
Height Loss: 750 metres

Birthday Dangling

Despite a poor night's sleep, I woke up singing at half past six the next morning, singing Happy Birthday that is. Esther had just completed another orbit around the sun and although we'd agreed that our fantastic summer of hiking was enough of a gift for each of us, I hoped that today's attempt at another high-altitude crossing might prove particularly special. Esther, for her part, told me that my no longer being in pain was the best gift.

Singing, tent folding and gear stuffing until just after seven, we sat in the shade of the mountain wrapped in our down jackets, eating breakfast and watching the pale moon set behind the peaks to our west. Away to our right the summit of Mont Blanc was clearly visible across 40 miles of purple morning sky. There were few clouds and only a light breeze, suggesting that we'd have perfect conditions for whatever unexpected challenges lay above us.

Bidding farewell to our neighbours and receiving a short Belgian version of Happy Birthday by way of a goodbye, we set out on our climb. Unusually for me, I was nervous about the challenge ahead. Not about the risk of the climb myself, but about whether it would go well and we'd actually enjoy it together. I didn't mind if we had to turn back, I was far more worried we'd get to the top and regret it.

Aiming for the sharp and jagged summit of Herbetet (3778 metres), we moved upwards through the stones and dirt scattered around the still grassy hillside. Cresting a steeper portion of trail, we emerged onto a slightly flatter area which gave us our first clear view of the valley head we would be climbing. The snow-dusted triangle of Herbetet still dominated the scene, dropping smoothly away to the left towards a small patch of glacier clinging to a ridgeline some 400-500 metres lower down, while to the right it sawed away more gradually, passing above a larger glacier and continuing right in a series of jagged teeth. According to our map, it was directly through those teeth that we had to pass at a point known as the Colle Gran Neyron, but try as we might we couldn't make out anything remotely trail-like in the almost vertical jumble of cliff face and scree beneath that imposing ridge. The rest of the valley head was the increasingly familiar chaos of white snow, dirty ice and heaps of grey detritus, but the climb we were supposed to attempt looked more like a wall than a hiking route.

The sun was just starting to touch the higher portions of the mountains when a thirteen-strong herd of nimble chamois appeared, grazing on the scrubby grass between us and the start of a grey moraine. That was the way we needed to go, once again following yellow stripes of paint as we left the grass behind and took to the stones.

The moraine was steep but not technically challenging, taking us a fair bit higher before dipping back into a small gorge in the rubble to our right. We still couldn't see a trail anywhere, so it was a case of one yellow marker at a time as we began picking a route uphill again, passing through larger and larger boulders and getting closer to the seemingly impassable cliff.

It was here that we realised the boulders we were hopping between were imbedded directly into the glacial ice. As we'd seen several times during the summer, the rubble had masked the lower portions of glacier until we were literally stood right on top of it. It was only then that we saw the start of the climb, with about a dozen metal footplates hammered directly into an otherwise blank rock face thirty metres above us.

The ground between us and the footplates had largely collapsed, leaving behind the aftermath of a mini rockslide. With our fingertips in the dusty remains we hauled ourselves doggedly towards the final yellow marker we could see, only to discover that because of the collapse a six-foot step was now required to reach the first footplate. I jumped first, just catching hold of the blue rope strung above the plates with a plan to pull Esther over behind me. It was at that moment that our camera decided to take a nose-dive south. Springing out of my hip pocket, it began bouncing away downhill only to get wedged between the tips of two enormous boulders that were almost touching. It was only about five metres below me, so near and yet so far.

I reckoned I could get it back, so I helped Esther across the gap to leave us sharing a couple of six-inch wide footplates above the fall below. It was a little tricky for a moment, but we managed to dance around each other and leave me able to scramble down to the camera. I couldn't believe how lucky we'd been. Two centimetres to the side and it would have been a hundred metres below us before we could have said the word "bollocks". As it was, apart from some new scratches and dents, it still worked. In fact, a recent "lens error" issue we'd been getting seemed to have even been resolved. Bonus.

Losing the camera wouldn't have been the end of the world, but pictures of our travels have always been an important part of our adventures. Esther has a real passion for capturing the world in images, which is lucky for me as I prefer bashing away at a keyboard. On that first interrail trip I mentioned, used camera films had been our most highly prized possession, even more so than passports and traveller's cheques (remember those?). This was long before smartphones and low-cost digital cameras, so instead we'd taken our collection of 36-exposure films with us everywhere in a very fetching red bumbag. As you can imagine, we didn't look like tourists at all.

By the time I'd walked across the footplates myself Esther was already making a start on the next series of obstacles. We were around 3100 metres altitude at this point, so only had about 200 vertical metres left to climb to the col. Yet although it was indeed a 'near-vertical' cliff, as with so many hiking routes, up close it wasn't so bad. Yes, there were narrow rock ledges, a surprisingly shaky metal ladder, several ropes and, higher up, quite a few thick metal chains to hang onto. Yes, there were occasional sheer drops down onto the glacier. And yes, some of the chain pulls did make us look like a 1960's version of Batman and Robin walking up the side of a building. But it wasn't a 'via ferrata', at least not in the sense that we understood the term. Without the aid of the chains and ropes some parts would have been scrambling to the point of climbing, but with them it was just good, solid hard work. And lots of fun.

Every time I looked up, or down, at Esther depending on which of us was leading, I was so proud of her. The same lady whose knees had once gone wobbly on a Lake District tourist motorway was now hauling herself up a chain, high above an Alpine glacier at over 3000 metres. All of which says nothing about the rest of the view. Pausing for breath occasionally on some of the wider ledges, we found ourselves looking down onto a magnificent glacial valley which flowed directly towards the distant splendour of the Mont Blanc massif.

A final few chain pulls up narrow ravines and we'd done it. The col itself was so tiny, just a metre-wide notch in the ridge, that it was as though we'd temporarily become part of the ridge itself. Earlier in the morning we'd looked up in awe and incredulity at the challenge we'd chosen, but now we were so high that we were on a level with almost everything around us. Everything, that is, apart from the mighty Gran Paradiso and its nearby sister summits which we were now able enjoy directly ahead of us.

We'd climbed to 3295 metres via one side of a sharp ridge and now the other side of the ridge revealed its treasures. To our right the ground fell away into a view that was open and far-reaching, stretching for hundreds of kilometres into both Italy and France, including the highest summits of the Vanoise National Park and quite possibly the Ecrins National Park as well. To our left, beyond a cairn decorated with colourful prayer flags, was a series of debris-filled and glaciated slopes reaching up towards the highest summits in the park. It was magnificent. After two hours of exhilarating climbing we paused to breathe in the freedom of this lofty perch. It was possibly the finest place we had reached all summer, with the Gran Paradiso on one side and the distance Mont Blanc massif on the other. That said, it's hard to compare 'perfect' with 'more perfect'.

We rested for only twenty minutes before starting our descent into the valley ahead of us. The downhill trail turned out to be much easier than the ascent and didn't require any ropes or chains, making us glad we'd tackled this pass in the direction that we had. We lost height slowly at first, passing beneath the ridge we'd just crossed and surprising a pair of sunbathing ibex that were lounging by the side of the track. Well, I say surprising. They woke up for about four seconds to look at us and then went back to sleep.

Eventually we began to move away from the shadow of the ridge, undulating over an open trail to cross the gently sloping mountainside. The sun was beating down powerfully by now, so it was no surprise to find the terrace at Rifugio F. Chabod (2750 metres) so busy with hikers and their beers when we reached it just after midday. These were the first other people we'd seen since setting out and there were hundreds of them all decked out in vibrantly coloured hiking gear. Some looked like day hikers but others looked like post-summit Gran Paradiso climbers. This refuge was one of several potential starting points for the climb and, if they had summitted, then they'd probably set out in the early hours of the morning, making this a well-earned rest for them. Looking up at some of the large glaciers flowing down from the tops, we could make out half a dozen tiny strands of climbers still making their way down.

The busyness and noise of the refuge was a bit of a shock to the system after such a thrilling but private experience, so we decided to carry on a little further before having our own lunch. We eventually came to rest twenty minutes later on a cluster of stones next to a small stream.

We ended up remaining static for over ninety minutes, taking a nap in the heat of the day and generally basking in the wondrous surroundings. We still had a potentially long distance to hike, but after the adrenalin of the morning we now felt little hurry to get going. Plus, there were blueberry bushes nearby!

According to our notes our next stop should be the humbly-named Rifugio Vittoria Emmanuel II (2735 metres), which we would reach after a long and fairly flat traverse around the large shoulder of rock to our left, followed by an 800 metre descent into the village of Pont at the end of the Valsavarenche valley. However, from our map we could see that the refuge was actually a detour and that there was a more direct route down to Pont, so that's ultimately what we decided to do.

It was a pretty walk down from our lunch stop into Pont, with a quiet, stony traverse followed by a busy and well-made trail downhill. We arrived into Pont by late afternoon, initially planning to stay on the campsite and complete our tour of Gran Paradiso the next morning. Our notes told us that we were now less than two and half hours away from returning to the Colle del Nivolet, just above the point at which Emilio and Paulo had dropped us off, with only a 300 metre climb out of Pont followed by a gentle stroll up the almost flat valley of Plan de Nivolet.

Yet when it turned out the campsite office was closed and we found ourselves twiddling our thumbs, we began to get other ideas. Reasoning that trying to get from

Pont all the way to Val d'Isere in a single day would be far too much, we began to wonder if we couldn't go a little further after all and make Val d'Isere an option? It would mean doing another 300 metre climb and a long flat trek to the next refuge, but it was only late afternoon. There was plenty of daylight left. Wasn't there?

The climb out of Pont was a series of well-made switchbacks where the main challenge was to get Esther to stop eating wild raspberries and crack on. She definitely got some birthday leeway though. Within just forty-five minutes we'd emerged onto the lower reaches of the Plan de Nivolet to find a landscape of gently rolling hillocks and tufty grass and we knew immediately that we'd made a big mistake.

The problem we had was that our Vanoise map and our Gran Paradiso map didn't quite overlap with each other, leaving just a small unknown void that was mostly taken up by the length of the Plan de Nivolet. Yet what we'd imagined as a short, flat trek based on altitude differences turned out to be a visibly extensive valley that was going to take at least another two hours of walking. Not hard walking, but a lot of walking nonetheless, and with seven hours in our legs already today, we suddenly knew it was beyond us. We'd misjudged our stamina and ability to go quicker than our notes.

The last thing we wanted to do was backtrack 300 metres downhill and have to come back up in the morning, but nor were we too keen on bending the wild camping rules again. In the end, however, our immediate fatigue won the day and dictated that we found a place to pitch our tent.

Fortunately, we found an ideal spot, an abandoned cow shed a couple of hundred metres to the side of the main trail with a relatively clean floor that we could put our tent up on. The roof looked a little flaky, but we reasoned that if it was going to collapse it would have done so fifty years ago. Being able to pop up just our inner-tent inside four stone walls made us feel much more secure and inconspicuous as we settled down for a warming bowl of couscous. Esther always tells me I take her to the best restaurants and this was her birthday after all.

I know some women wouldn't want to sleep in a cowshed on their birthday (or at all), but I'm a lucky man in more ways than one. Sat on our temporary doorstep, we gazed back across the sunset coloured Valsavarenche valley and the intricate beauty of the Gran Paradiso massif. Every step we had taken since crossing the magnificent Colle Gran Neyron was rolled out in front of us, threading across the scene beneath those lofty summits. It had been a dazzling day. A big day, and one that had put us within just a couple of hours of completing a tour all the way around that beautiful giant. The eastern sky was already deep blue, fading to black, and as that curtain rolled slowly over the top of us we found ourselves lying back on the stones to appreciate the stars. Could life really be this simple?

Vital Statistics – Day 12
Start: Below Colle Gran Neyron
End: Plan de Nivolet
Distance Hiked: 18 kilometres
Hiking Time: 7 hours
Height Gain: 1090 metres
Height Loss: 1440 metres

Back to France

The glimmering moon rose shortly after sunset, lighting the scene in glorious monochrome and banishing all but the brightest stars from the sky. Tucked away in our mesh-like inner-tent I was aware of the brightness outside, but it was Esther who got the full show. Unable to sleep, she spent several hours lying beneath the stars in just her sleeping bag while the Earth's little sister walked across the sky.

Morning bought an even greater treat when a family of marmots appeared from a burrow entrance just ten metres from our own temporary doorway. With a lone adult standing guard, three cubs play-wrestled on the grass without a care in the world. They could obviously see us but must have decided we weren't much of a threat as the adult continued to maintain its statuesque pose. When a vulture flew high above us, the adult chirruped loudly and the cubs vanished in just half a second. All along the valley we could hear the warning being echoed by other guarding marmots. It was five minutes until they re-emerged and began wrestling again.

Sitting on the doorstep with our abandoned cow-shed looking like a rustic farmhouse behind us, it felt like we were home. We didn't need to say anything, just hold each and look out over peaks and valleys, snow and grass, beauty and power. We sat for over twenty minutes watching the scene, with the marmots playing and the sun rising in the sky. In a sense, today was a job to get done. It was time to retrace our steps back over the Col de la Lose and return to France and the Vanoise National Park.

Most of what we would walk would be familiar territory but it didn't feel in the least bit uninspiring. On the contrary, I was excited to experience it all again on a different day and to see just how much had changed in a week. We'd first climbed the Col de la Lose in snow but I doubted that any of it had hung around during the past five days of hot weather. What new sights would we be able to see? Would it feel the same? What had we already forgotten?

Our initial route took us back to the main trail and then south along the almost completely flat floor of the Plan de Nivolet. With a handful of small, gentle streams flowing around us and the shallow sides of the valley rising up towards smooth crags, this was a far softer landscape than we'd been used to around the rest of our Gran Paradiso tour. A handful of higher peaks beyond the shallow valley head were topped with white, their height marking the border with France and the Vanoise.

We had only 200 metres of ascent to reach the Rifugio Citta di Chivasso, from where we would descend back to Lago Serru, but we still had a chunky amount of distance to cover and it was proving surprisingly tiring. The trail was easy underfoot and there were no obstacles greater than an occasional pebble or puddle to overcome, but it didn't feel quite as easy as it should do. Obviously, we were feeling the hangover from our six days of boulder fields, ups, downs and 3000 metre passes.

It took us almost two hours in the end to reach the refuge at 2604 metres, where a somewhat ramshackle exterior hid a unique and cosy shelter like no other refuge we'd ever seen. With just 34 beds it was a relatively small place, but the book-lined main dining room felt more like a library than a mountain hut. A tower-like blue ceramic stove stood at the centre of the main room, while old skis and other historic mountain paraphernalia (even a stuffed raven) were perched around the walls or jammed between the books. It looked like a very snug place to spend an evening and the staff couldn't have been friendlier, even digging out one of their own phone chargers for us when our own adapter failed to fit in the socket.

Sitting outside on a bench and eating refuge-purchased oranges, there was definitely a lethargy hanging over us. Perhaps it was because we'd just finished a tour of the Gran Paradiso in just over six days and we were just physically tired, but I expect it also had a mental element as well. There was a sense that something was coming to end. We expected to have at least four more days of walking before getting back to our motorhome, or maybe five if we dragged it out now that we'd gone so fast around Gran Paradiso, but then what? Driving. Motorways. Cities. People. It just didn't seem real after a summer of hillsides and air mattresses, marmots and ibex, peaks and valleys, snow and ice. Yet the completion of this milestone bought that alternative reality onto the fringe of our awareness, at least for a while.

The melancholy didn't last long though. Four days is still a lot of walking and we soon shook off the heaviness as we jogged down the tarmac switchbacks towards Lago Serru. Pausing only once to take a quick photo of the corner where Paulo and Emilio had dropped us off in the freezing fog, looking very different and far more hospitable now in the sunshine, we soon picked up a dirt track and began rising above the surface of that familiar lake. We couldn't help smiling at the memory of ourselves a week earlier. There had been so much lying in store for us. So many challenges and moments of joy as yet unknown. So many smiles. Where had the time gone? It was enough to make a man get philosophical!

Sometimes I think nostalgia is really just fear of the unknown. We idealise certain moments in our past because we know how things worked out and we know there were good. Student heydays. Family events. Sporting victories. Sometimes we think we want to relive them but we also forget how, at the time, we were just as uncertain or lost in our thoughts as we are today. We didn't know how it would turn out so we were scared, or we took it for granted, or we were too busy worrying about homework to realise how great it was.

Nostalgia, for me, is really just a reminder to live in the moment. Whatever comes next can hold just as much joy and happiness as our mental highlights do, and it will be much richer if we can remember to fully enjoy it while it's happening instead of looking back and enjoying it second-hand from some uncertain future perspective.

Setting my eyes towards the five hundred metres of climbing that would take us back to France, we began rising more steeply. The D-rings and cables on the cliffs above the Plan della Ballotta bivacco seemed much more extensive than I recalled from our descent. The drops seemed much more precipitous now that we were going up, as did the severity of the dusty switchbacks and the chain-assisted sections immediately beneath the col. We'd been over some precarious passes around Gran Paradiso, so it had been easy to forget these short but demanding challenges required to get from one park to the next.

There was one big difference though, the weather. Reaching the col we were no longer confronted with a snow-packed valley head and icicles that we could use as light sabres, but a summer-like panorama of sun-soaked valleys and shiny slopes. A smattering of clouds cast their long shadows over the hillsides and there was a cold breeze gusting over the col, but with everything between the summit of Gran Paradiso and the summit of La Grande Casse visible in the early afternoon light, our heads were literally spinning in an attempt to take it all in.

We stopped for lunch on the col, falling asleep in the small wind-shelter provided by the slope, before readying ourselves for a quick trek back down towards Val d'Isere. The trail back down to Refuge de Prariond was clear, easy-to-follow and brief as we found ourselves practically jogging back down into the Vanoise, a very different experience to the snow-hidden path we'd forged uphill on our last visit to this valley. On our right were green hills and grey cliffs, to our left were coal-dark scree slopes and in the centre of it all, twinkling at us through the valley's opening, were the sunny rooftops of Val d'Isere coaxing us forward. The pace we'd set from the col was firm and we maintained that pace right through the flat portion of the valley, past all of the beautiful purple flowers lining the path and all the way down to the road at Pont St-Charles, which we reached in less than an hour from the col, a 900 metre descent.

Our intention for the evening, we'd agreed, was to bivouac somewhere outside of the Vanoise National Park boundary and the parking at Pont St-Charles was our first such opportunity. There was a perfect flat spot hidden behind a small mound of gravel by the river's edge, plus a dry-toilet we could use in the car park. But it didn't feel right somehow. It was only just after four and there was still ample daylight left to walk a little further. Or at least that's what we said out loud as we began the few kilometres of tarmac walking towards Val d'Isere.

The truth was, although neither of us was admitting it to each other, we both had the lure of the Hotel Avancher down in Val d'Isere tugging at the back of our minds. It had been such a deeply comfortable, luxurious experience the last time around that we couldn't shake the idea that we might, just possibly, stay there again. Yet it also felt wastefully extravagant. We weren't wet this time, but warm, and there were definitely no -5°C temperatures forecast for the night ahead. Plus, we only had a few more days of hiking left until we got back to our motorhome. We obviously didn't really *need* to stay there again, which is why we weren't saying it to each other. But the idea was there, teasing us, tempting us to spoil ourselves.

We didn't really even need to stop in Val d'Isere. We still had enough supplies with us from Cogne and we'd be passing through another ski-town the next day, Tignes-le-Lac, which would almost certainly have places to buy food. However, we still stopped briefly at the supermarket directly opposite the Hotel Avancher for a few fresh items. I went in first and came out with a perfectly ripe avocado, a juicy tomato and a half-litre bottle of freshly-squeezed orange juice, all of which we ate immediately outside the store. Then, when Esther popped back in for a small carton of coconut milk to go with dinner, I quickly switched on her phone to check Booking.com.

Disappointingly, the Hotel Avancher had no available rooms listed for the night ahead. All that was showing in Val d'Isere were a couple of rooms in the 'other' hotel, the one that we'd not chosen the last time around. Esther came back out just as I was switching the phone off, so I told her that I'd checked anyway and there weren't any rooms.

"I know" she replied. "I looked while you were in the shop."

We laughed, partly at ourselves for being so sneaky, and also because we were fifty metres away from a hotel but checking availability online instead of just going in. How depressingly modern and disconnected of us.

"Why don't we ask anyway?" I said, "just to see how much they have rooms for". It was only when we crossed the road that we noticed a sheet of A4 taped up just inside the main doors. Turned out the Hotel Avancher had also closed until the winter season started, and just a day after we'd left the last time. All that fuss and wondering and we couldn't have stayed even if we'd wanted to, which set us laughing again.

We didn't even consider the other hotel but did go into the tourist office to ask for advice on where we might bivouac nearby. The staff were busy working on posters and leaflets for the Christmas market when we arrived and seemed slightly surprised to see any visitors at all. They were also very apologetic about the fact that everything but a single hotel and a half-stocked supermarket had closed until the ski season. In terms of bivouac advice, they gave us a few suggestions and said that as long as we were out of the town areas we'd be very unlikely to get disturbed at this time of year.

It was coming up to six o'clock when we left Val d'Isere and our intention was to rejoin the "Tour of the Vanoise" guidebook itinerary by picking up the GR5 trail towards Tignes-le-Lac. That would take us out of town and onto a tree-lined hillside where we felt sure we'd find a good place to camp.

In the end we didn't even have to walk that far, which was good because unbeknownst to us at the time we'd just completed our longest day of hiking of the entire summer, marching twenty-eight kilometres in just six hours. Until I sat down to write this book we hadn't a clue quite how far we'd come. Thankfully, we'd only just left Val d'Isere when we came across a tangle of small streams running through the trees to the left of the trail. Something about the spot just felt right to us, so we decided to walk upstream a short way. In just fifty metres we were surrounded by a young pine forest that gave us good shelter from both the main trail and the town and had a nice soft floor of pine needles. It was perfect. This was where we would camp for the night.

Collecting a little water from one of the streams, I set about preparing some quinoa with curry spices and the coconut milk Esther had bought us, while Esther went off for an explore. Ten minutes later she came back looking excited and said "It's amazing. I've found treehouse."

"A treehouse?" I said uncertainly. "You mean a little hut up in a tree?"

"Yes. It's great. It has a sofa in it and everything. I think maybe we can sleep in it."

"Well, how far away is it?" I asked dubiously. I'd only just sat down and had no desire to traipse uphill again.

"Maybe a hundred metres. You can almost see it, just there" she said, pointing and still looking excited.

So we moved, juggling a pan of half-cooked quinoa through a maze of streams and fallen trees in search of the treehouse that Esther seemed to have already forgotten the way to.

"That's not a treehouse!" I declared when we reached it. "It's on the bloody ground."

"But it is in a tree" Esther threw back. "And it's not on the ground on this side, it's on stilts."

"Having a tree at each corner doesn't count as 'in a tree'" I said, raising my eyebrows, "and those stilts are less than two-feet tall."

There then followed a short, pointless and very light-hearted debate about what, in fact, a treehouse was. None of which mattered because it seemed that our accommodation for the night had just improved.

The cabin, which we agreed to call a treehouse because Esther had once had a childhood dream of sleeping in a treehouse, was about four metres square, three metres tall and built out of the most eclectic mix of building materials you can imagine. The walls were made of everything from chipboard to metal panels, while the floor inside was a jigsaw of offcuts in a rainbow of different colours. The roof was made out of wooden panels covered with tarpaulin, though it also had a series of corrugated metal sheets propped up on questionable supports in what looked like an effort to create a sloping roof. There were no windows but there was a door, albeit a door that was too small to fill the door-shaped hole in the wall. There was a six-inch gap down the side of the 'door' and a two-foot gap above it, leaving the inside essentially open to the elements. There really was a sofa though, a big brown one, plus a table, four orange plastic chairs and a wooden box full of tools and tins of beer.

Outside, a strange mix of half-built pallet-furniture, a barbeque and a swing were scattered around. The overall impression was that this was something built by grown men who wanted a place in the woods to hang out and drink beer, but who had gotten bored and started drinking the beer before finishing their den. Either that, or they'd be back later. I mean, some serious work had obviously gone into this cabin, sorry, 'treehouse'. Even getting the materials here would have involved carrying a lot of very heavy things at least five hundred metres from the nearest dirt road.

We decided to risk it and stay inside. If anyone did show up we were sure they wouldn't mind a couple of hikers sleeping on their floor. If they wanted extra security they should have built a door that fitted the hole in the wall. Besides, I even mended a few things for them, clambering onto the roof and re-assembling the corrugated sheets of metal that had been blown into a creaking, haphazard heap. There was no way I could sleep with that racket going on every time the breeze wafted through the trees.

While I was being manly up on the roof, Esther was being a home-maker (how traditional) and rearranging the sofa cushions into a good approximation of a double-bed on the floor. By the time I came down she'd even rolled out our sleeping bags to create our own little nest in the woods for the night. Yes, the cabin was open to the elements. No, we didn't know if anyone was going to show up with a six-pack and a saw. But in that moment, when the sky began to turn pale pink and all we could hear was the sound of trees swaying in the wind, it was an ocean of tranquillity that was all our own.

We spent the twilight hour taking turns on the rope swing before sitting on the porch to watch the remainder of the sunset. The porch, incidentally, was one of the most well-finished parts of the whole construction, as though the builders had gotten lazier the higher they'd built. The steps up to it, for example, were a masterpiece.

Laying down in our sleeping bags in pitch darkness, with the nocturnal sounds of the woods outside and a soft breeze still tickling our cheeks, we felt exposed, but we also felt perfectly at home again. How fortunate that the Hotel Avancher had been closed after all. It was a perfect example of how when one door closes, another opens, because as nice as another trip to the spa would have been it wouldn't have been half as special as this.

Vital Statistics – Day 13
Start: Plan de Nivolet
End: A 'treehouse' in Val d'Isere
Distance Hiked: 28 kilometres
Hiking Time: 6 hours
Height Gain: 990 metres
Height Loss: 1740 metres

In the Heart

Nobody showed up to disturb us in the night, or even in the morning come to that. I was a little alarmed when I woke up to the sound of rumbling engines apparently coming towards our nest, but it was only trucks on a distant access road. For a moment I thought the people who'd built the hut had decided to knock it down and have another go.

Reassembling our bed into a sofa, we brewed up a morning saucepan of tea and some warm porridge with the last of our food, before sitting in suburban comfort to look out of our misshapen door. After so much wilderness, I felt tremendously civilised to be sitting on a sofa with a brew. I could have sat there all morning as the sun climbed higher and the air outside began to slowly warm up.

Our route away from the cabin followed the GR5 uphill and west away from Val d'Isere. There was a little confusion over which of the many tracks threading through the trees was actually the GR5 and we did get lost for a while. However, the presence of an access road heading up towards the ski lift stations above La Daille gave us an easy orientation marker and we were soon back on the right track.

Our route today was a discrete stage from the "Tour of the Vanoise" guidebook, a six hour, eighteen kilometre trek from Val d'Isere to the Refuge de la Leisse. with 1110 metres of ascent thrown in for good measure. It had been a while since we could be that exact about our route. When we'd first crossed into Italy we didn't even have a map.

The valley we were currently walking up, the Vallon de le Tovière, was an open green hillside with a very mild gradient as we climbed towards the high point at the Pas de la Tovière. To our left the peculiarly shaped ridges of the Pointe du Lavachet looked almost like cement that had been poured from a great height before setting too fast in the hot sun. The exposed rock was bright white, like chalk, which stood out starkly against the rest of the landscape.

During the climb we passed several sheep and a fairly large herd of horses grazing freely on the grass. As we left the extensive sight of Val d'Isere behind us it was temporarily easy to forget that we were, in fact, surrounded by the industry of winter leisure. For a time, all we could see was the slowly rising hillside around us and the tops of distant mountains, including Mont Blanc with its summit wrapped in thick white clouds.

Unfortunately, the illusion of pastoral remoteness was abruptly shattered when we crossed the Pas de la Tovière. Suddenly, in the valley below us, were the sprawling hotels and apartment blocks of Tignes-le-Lac. I'm not usually inclined to slag off ski-resorts and ski-lifts, as some other authors do, reasoning that they provide a service that allows people to spend time in beautiful places without the need to walk for days and camp. That said, Tignes-le-Lac was definitely at the eyesore end of the spectrum.

With grey mountain tops and green hillside rising far above the brown, black and white multi-storey buildings of the town, some of them seven or eight storeys tall at least, it had not exactly been built to blend in. Away from the central huddle, a handful of especially large hotels were positioned like satellites orbiting the concrete hub.

Surprisingly, the view on the ground wasn't that bad. Once we arrived in the town centre the overall impression was of a relatively clean and modern place with a lovely outlook in all directions, which only goes to show how important perspective is I suppose. I'm not saying that Tignes-le-Lac isn't an ugly smudge in an otherwise stunning valley, but it isn't a litter-infested, horn-blaring chaos either. Although that's only our experience out of season.

And indeed, like Val d'Isere, it was very much out of season. We'd counted on finding a supermarket to buy supplies for the rest of our trip, but the first two we tried were firmly closely for the foreseeable future. We only had one left to try, so were massively relieved when the Carrefour Montagne was still open.

It had taken us two hours of hiking to make it here, and we'd only had a small breakfast, so we were very ready for a substantial meal. Sending my chief huntress into the store, I did the hard job of guarding our packs on a nearby sunny bench while I waited for the feast to arrive. And arrive it did, in style. Several reduced-price salad bowls, a loaf of nut and raisin bread and some dark chocolate covered rice cakes went a good distance towards filling the hole inside my belly. In fact, arguably, they over-filled it again. However, as we continued to sit in the sun and wait until we felt energetic enough to shop for longer term supplies, I didn't mind in the least. We had plenty of daylight left and felt in no massive hurry to get moving again.

Tignes-le-Lac sits, as you might have guessed, on the edge of a large lake called (inventively) Lac de Tignes. The original village of Tignes was actually built much lower in the valley but was flooded out in the 1950s when the Barrage de Tignes was built, creating a huge reservoir known today as the Lac du Chevril. This new, modern replacement was specifically positioned to take best advantage of the skiing opportunities on the surrounding slopes.

Coupled with Val d'Isere and the village of Val Claret, which we would shortly walk towards, there are over 97 ski lifts and 300 kilometres of pistes in the region, plus a funicular railway that can take people all the way to a restaurant at 3030 metres on a spire of rock above La Grande Motte's glacier. From there, visitors can then hop on a téléphérique all the way up to 3450 metres, just 200 metres below the summit of La Grande Motte itself.

Somehow, despite the existence of the funicular and téléphérique, and the fact that it can be used for year-round skiing, the surface of the glacier has been named the Réserve Naturelle de Tignes. From our position just at the edge of the lake (which is the most peaceful and beautiful part of Tignes by the way), we could just about see the edge of the glacier above the high-rise apartments of Val Claret. On the lake itself we could see a number of boats pootling around and a paddle-boarder making her way around the edge. Again, looking up was a most majestic view. It was only when the eye was drawn to the extensive, multi-storey apartments in Tignes or Val Claret, or the ear tuned in to the distant sound of cranes and reversing trucks continuing to build even more of them, that the illusion was broken.

It was just a short walk around the edge of the lake and then a little further along a gravel path to Val Claret. Bearing in mind this was only mid-September, it was quite a surprise to find workmen hanging Christmas decorations on all of the lampposts we passed as we walked into town. Of course, since this entire place also seemed to be closed, we supposed it was the most sensible time of year to do it. Far better than trying to put them up when it's actually cold and snowing. It was downright roasting when we got there, not to mention dusty. In fact, we even got to see a twenty metre high tornado kicking up the dust in one of the large, empty car parks around the edge of town, which isn't something you see very often. It was a very beautiful and elegant sight.

Still, it was quite a relief when we found the edge of the GR55 trail climbing out of Val Claret and began heading directly back towards the Vanoise National Park boundary. We'd had enough of ski lifts and deserted apartment buildings for now and were looking forward to another dose of mountain solitude, or companionship depending on how busy the refuge was. Since the refuge we were heading towards was on the main Cicerone guide route, we expected it would probably be quite well occupied, as most of the others had been earlier in our tour. It was only the Refuge de la Femma that had been quiet and that hadn't been on the main itinerary but part of an optional variant.

Initially following the line of a pair of ski-lifts constructed just outside of the park boundary, we eventually began veering right in the direction of the icy summit of La Grande Motte, crossing back into the Vanoise at over 2500 metres. By now the clouds on the horizon had cleared slightly and we could easily make out the bulk of the entire Mont Blanc massif in the north, while immediately around us was a tundra of crags and beige, sun-bleached grass. Ahead of us was our high point for the day, the Col de la Leisse at 2761 metres, but the slope was so gradual either side of the col that had there not been a sign it would have been hard to mark the exact moment we crossed it.

We now had an excellent view of the impressive La Grande Motte glacier and the out-of-place pylons that supported the surprising presence of that téléphérique. It was the only remaining hint of human development we could see up here, back in the park and surrounded by near total nature once more.

We began the ninety-minute descent to the refuge with excited (but still sore) feet, eager to stop for the day and put up our tent in this delightful scenery. After the severe climbs of our Gran Paradiso loop, there was a noticeable shift in the physical demands of these more frequently used trails. They were wider and gentler in a way that matched the softer landscape. There were still bare summits, glaciers and sheer drops around us, but none of it seemed as plunging or abrupt. It felt more mellow, not just in terms of gradient, but overall. Or perhaps it was just our mood that day.

We skirted along one brilliant blue lake before descending a little more and skirting a peculiarly flat and spartan bowl where our map indicated another larger lake should be. Yet it wasn't there. It had apparently vanished, probably the result of the narrow opening in the corner being un-dammed, or so we guessed. It did allow us to go straight across the dried mud of the former lake-bottom though, saving us a little time, before rounding a small rock pinnacle to find the refuge waiting for us in the afternoon sun.

Sited at 2487 metres on the sloping green hillside, we could see immediately that this refuge had a very special outlook that stretched right along the Vallon de la Leisse. In front of the refuge the ground fell away sharply, creating an ideal viewpoint to appreciate the steep and rounded sides of the valley. Bearing in mind that the northern flank of the valley stretches up to the highest peak in the entire park, La Grande Casse at 3865 metres, you can imagine the scale of the view afforded to this wonderful thirty-two-bed refuge.

But where was everyone? There wasn't a soul around and most of the doors were closed and shuttered. There were three buildings, or four if you count the small toilet block. Each of the main buildings was a wooden construction with a sharply triangular roof covering low walls, a little like big wooden tents really. One was the reception/guardian's office which was shuttered and padlocked, while the dortoir and the dining room were shuttered but unlocked. We let ourselves into both, discovering in each an alarming state of neatness with all crockery smartly stacked, tables scrubbed, pillows lined up and blankets expertly folded. Apparently, the refuge had already closed for winter!

That many refuges leave open a "winter room" for out-of-season use is a fantastic facility. In a world so often marred by suspicion and the belief that people will abuse trust if given the chance, refuges simply leave a part of their

164

buildings unlocked and ask for payments to be posted in an honesty box. How great is that?

We were the only people here so far and while we'd planned to camp outside, for the sake of the eleven euros each "winter" dormitory fee we immediately changed those plans to a night on a foam mattress instead.

The dining room was spacious and supplied with various books and magazines in several languages, so after a spot of fresh salad and some bread for dinner, we agreed to each take a little time to unwind in the relative luxury we'd stumbled into. On the walls of the dining room were breathtaking pictures of the surrounding hillsides taken by local photographers, including some of wolves, while a French version of the age-old "weather-forecasting stone" was hanging by the door. Maybe you've seen one before? It's a nice way to poke fun at the intricacy and unreliability of modern forecasts. The one of in the Refuge de la Leisse came with following options:

> stone wet – raining
> stone dry – fine
> stone invisible – fog
> stone shiny – ice
> stone white – snow
> stone moving – windy
> stone missing – hurricane
> two stones – go to bed!!!

I picked an English language fiction book and settled on the sofa for an hour of uninterrupted reading, while Esther chose to sit outside and simply breathe in the expansive scenery while the sun began to dip in the sky.

As twilight was setting in, about seven o'clock, I suddenly heard a startled shriek from Esther and dashed outside to find her fussing a large, shaggy, brown and white dog. The dog was clearly enjoying himself but the moment

I called out to Esther he took one look at me and ran away. Esther explained that she'd been sitting quietly when something suddenly licked her ear from behind, which is when she'd cried out. Thinking it was me playing a trick on her, she'd instead turned to find herself nose-to-snout with the forward visitor. Where he'd come from and where he was going, we hadn't a clue. We guessed there must have been a shepherd nearby but we hadn't seen anyone.

At least it gave me a reason to join Esther and take in what was left of the sunset together before we began to get ready for bed. Nobody else had turned up and it looked like we were going to have the entire place to ourselves for the night after all, which was a bit of a thrill. Not that we would have minded sharing, but getting our own collection of wooden huts for the night complete with a kitchen and toilet was certainly a step up in the world.

What we couldn't get our heads around was that so much had changed in just over a week. We'd started out from Pralognan to find full refuges, friends and camaraderie. Now things were shutting down. Was it really so late in the season? If anything, the weather had been improving, so it didn't feel like it, despite the noticeably earlier sunset.

Vital Statistics – Day 14
Start: A 'treehouse' in Val d'Isere
End: Refuge de la Leisse
Distance Hiked: 18 kilometres
Hiking Time: 6 hours
Height Gain: 1110 metres
Height Loss: 430 metres

Finishing

A clear night marked by possibly the finest display of stars and the galactic arc of the Milky Way we'd ever seen preceded our fifteenth day of continuous hiking. You get to see a lot of beautiful night skies in the high mountains, a gift of the clear air and low levels of light pollution, but until the moon rose in the early hours we were treated to something very special at Refuge de la Leisse. A dazzling display of galactic awesomeness which, combined with the hulking silhouettes of mountains, really hammered home our human frailty in the vastness of the universe. It made us feel blessed to be alive and sharing in this rare treat.

We were now just a single guidebook stage away from our motorhome, a mere six hour effort over seventeen kilometres, with just 420 metres of climbing and a more demanding 1490 metres of descent. The question was, did we really want to finish today? Or did we want to find a way to eke it out? Perhaps stay at the refuge before the final descent, the Refuge du Col de la Vanoise, or break off in another direction entirely?

The question caused a certain amount of friction between us because, for my part, I felt ready to stop. Yes, we'd gone so quickly that we still had a few days in hand, but with more than six weeks of summer hiking under my belt, I couldn't see anything on the map that inspired me to add on extra loops or climbs for the sake of it. Esther, on the hand, was reluctant for the tour to end. She still wanted 'one more night', if she could get it. I could understand that, but it didn't change my mind.

Thankfully, while we respected that we had slightly different preferences, we also knew that it didn't really matter. We'd had a fabulous summer and one or two days either way wasn't going to change that. In the end, we decided to just start the walk and see what arose. It was an approach that had always worked before and that we'd learned during our travels. Sometimes, trying to control everything saps so much energy that it just isn't worth it. Just getting started and seeing what life has in store often leads to far more exciting adventures.

Refolding the blankets we'd used as pillows, it took just a few minutes to return our private, sixteen-bunk dormitory (half of the refuge's beds) to the state we'd found it in before locking up behind us. After a brief breakfast, I popped down to the loo and by the time I came out there was an enormous pastou staring at me. Not barking, just standing silently and panting. I couldn't see any sheep nearby and the dog seemed docile so I stood still and let it approach me, slowly holding out the palm of hand, which the dog sniffed before letting me fuss her. Fussing a relaxed pastou is a bit like fussing a small friendly polar bear. It's brilliant. After a few seconds she was really getting into the fuss so I started calling for Esther to come and enjoy saying hello, but try as I might I couldn't get her attention.

The reason, I'd soon find out, was because Esther was around the other side of the refuge with her own dog for company. A young shepherdess had shown up at the refuge to take a look at the magazines in the dining room, bringing with her three of her five dogs. They'd gotten chatting and by the time I arrived were deep into an explanation of the shepherding life.

Juliet was about our age and had been shepherding for almost ten years. The herd she looked after had five hundred sheep in it and belonged to two brothers from a nearby valley. In the early grazing season, the brothers stayed with the herd, but from July to the end of October it was Juliet's turn. We could see the herd drifting steadily west on the other side of the valley. At night Juliet slept in a small hut (which the park authorities move from time to time) and during the day she tends her flock, checking for

168

injuries and generally being on hand in case she was needed. Of her five dogs, two were pastou and mostly stayed with the sheep, the collie was for herding and the other two were just good company.

The shaggy brown and white dog from the night before, we discovered, was one of hers. The refuge had only closed three days earlier and all summer long the brown and white dog had been coming along after dinner for scraps from Justin, the chef, who had become a firm friend. Yet for the past three days the dog had been disappointed at finding nothing but an empty building after his long walk down for food.

"He must have been so excited to see you" Juliet said. "He must have been expecting food when he licked your ear."

It sounded like a solitary life for Juliet, but she said she loved feeling like a part of the mountain. She'd studied mountain geology and agriculture at college and to her, shepherds were as much part of Alpine life as the ibex, the herds and the wolves who might prey on them. Her partner, she told us, was also a shepherd and her main decision at the moment was whether they would shepherd a thousand-sheep herd together next year. Amazing as it sounds to a lay-person, she felt that 500 sheep was a very manageable number for one person, but with a thousand sheep it was hard even for two people to really 'know' the flock. Also, so many sheep together had a greater impact on the hillside and required more work and movement to make it sustainable.

She invited us to spend a day walking with the sheep alongside her, to see what her life was really like. It was a tempting offer and I could see Esther's eyes twinkling at the image of being a shepherdess herself. Esther loves and animals and the outdoors, so it seemed an ideal job in some ways, but in the end we declined. We felt ready to move on again and we also really wanted to enjoy each other's' company for the final days of our tour. Juliet also had to get moving to catch up with her sheep, who by now were a good couple of kilometres away and some distance above us. They couldn't get too far away, she'd explained, as there had been a recent wolf sighting in the area and at night she was having to build a corral for them as a result.

It was overcast when we set off but it didn't look likely to rain very soon. After a quick descent immediately below the refuge, the trail soon levelled off along the almost flat valley. We were heading towards an almost perfect V-shaped intersection of slopes ahead of us, formed by the lower reaches of La Grande Casse cutting from the right and from the slopes of the Pointes de Pierre Brune cutting in from the left. Rising up above the bottom of the 'V' was the slightly skewed triangle of the Pointe de la Rechasse (3212 metres), creating a stereotypical mountain scene reminiscent of something a child would draw at school. Somewhere up there, hidden on the right, was the trail that would take us up to the Col de la Vanoise.

A host of cows were strung out along the track as we walked and the valley began to curve gently left. As we got closer, we could see that a number of the scree slopes on our right still covered persistent glacial ice. There were even a few ice bridges spanning the Torrent de la Leisse which flowed down the centre of the valley.

Our first destination was the bridge of Pont de Croé-Vie at around 2100 metres, a bridge that dates back to the 16th century when it sat on an important salt trading route. This was the point at which we would begin the climb to the refuge and it was also the point at which the main tour of the Vanoise almost doubles back on itself, coming within less than a kilometre of the route we'd taken up to the Refuge de la Femma.

As we rounded the bend in the valley everything looked suddenly familiar, transporting us straight back to that happy time, just eleven days earlier, when we'd come down a nearby slope eating fresh blueberries with our friends Renee and Menno close behind. Except, of course, it wasn't really us that had come down that slope. It was two other people, earlier versions of ourselves that hadn't yet negotiated the boulder fields of the Gran Paradiso, or trekked in the sleet to Bivacco Giraudo, or even knocked on the door of a stone building to make friends with some hospitable Italian engineers. Had it really been only eleven days?

Crossing the Torrent de la Leisse via the historic stone bridge, we began the climb towards the Col de la Vanoise. Blueberry bushes surrounded the trail but in the days that we'd been gone the fruit had shrivelled and started to rot, making it hard to muster even a handful of the tasty ripeness we'd enjoyed so abundantly before. As we climbed, the view back up the Vallon de la Leisse grew increasingly spectacular while around us the hillside became more autumnal, the leaves shading to vibrant reds and yellows which made a blunt contrast against the dull grey of the rock walls far above.

A little higher still and we passed a memorial to two soldiers who had died nearby, followed a short while later by a concrete bunker with gun emplacements at either end. We could see the thick metal door of the bunker was jammed open, so with a grim fascination we slipped on our head torches and stepped into the dark to explore.

What we discovered was an eerie underground burrow, with a single narrow room perhaps twenty metres long covered with a curved and corrugated metal roof that connected the two round gun turrets. The gun emplacements each had a couple of square, tapered openings in the wall, giving a panoramic sweep over the entire valley below the bunker. Back in the connecting room there were plenty of wires and bits of tangled metal jutting out of the walls, suggesting equipment had once filled the space, but also lots of 21st century litter on the floor to show that we were far from the first people to come here recently. Most likely, some hikers even slept here we supposed.

From outside, only the slits of the gun emplacements and just a little concrete was visible. A web search told me that the bunker was most likely built by France between the two world wars to try and deter an invasion from Italy. No doubt life in this tiny concrete space would have been harsh and cold, especially in winter.

After our little subterranean adventure we carried on climbing beneath a darkening sky. The climbing didn't last much longer though before the trail veered left and entered another long, almost flat hanging valley which would take us most of the rest of the way to the refuge. With the imposing Pointe Mathews (3783 metres) on our right, a summit just to the side of La Grande Casse, and the Pointe de la Rechasse on our left, we were now walking into what the guidebook described as some of the greatest scenery of the entire tour. Peaks surrounded us on all sides while another garden of intricate cairns lined the path as we ventured deeper into the heart of the national park, directly beneath its highest summit.

We arrived at the Refuge du Col de la Vanoise after a solid three hours of walking, finding the largest refuge in the park (148 beds) still very much open for business with a busy restaurant doing a good trade. Based on the gear laid out to dry outside, there were climbers from La Grande Casse here alongside day hikers and the remnants of the season's tour walkers like us. A real mixed bunch you might say, but all united in their appreciation of this special place. The view up towards La Grande Casse was simply marvellous, revealing its glaciated upper slopes and exposed cliffs with crystal clarity. The sheer size of the mountainside as it towered over the refuge was amazing.

This was our decision time. Less than two hours downhill was the end of our tour and the relative comfort of our motorhome. On this hillside was the chance to continue our adventure for a short while longer. But which did we want?

Just as we'd expected, it was circumstances that made up our minds for us. The decisive factor came when we discovered the refuge was one of the few which didn't allow camping outside. They had plenty of spaces left and we were welcome to two of them. However, after the delight of our own private dortoir the night before we'd been somewhat spoiled in terms of shared sleeping spaces. The prospect of spending what could be our last night together in the mountains in a noisy bunkhouse did not fill me with enthusiasm.

Our tour, it seemed, would end today after all. And not just our tour, but our entire hiking summer. It was both a sad and a happy moment as that realisation dawned on us. We'd 'done' it, but it was also over. It had been amazing, but it was no more. It couldn't be taken away from us, but it couldn't continue either. Mixed emotions welled up inside of us as we held each other and decided not to even try and make sense of what we were feeling. Whatever it was would be the right thing.

Esther did briefly toy with the idea of a hike up to the Pointe de la Rechasse just because she could, but in the end decided against it because of the gathering clouds. A cluster had already drifted onto La Grande Casse and there seemed little point in a 700 metre ascent if there wasn't going to be much of a view. So we had lunch instead, a final warm saucepan of couscous followed by nuts and dried fruit, then a last hillside doze beneath the shifting patches of sun and shade.

We started our descent in late afternoon. The threatening clouds hadn't produced any of the wet stuff yet and even seemed to be slowly clearing as we walked west, heading beneath the crags of the Aiguille de la Vanoise and snaking down the steep slope towards the woods above Pralognan. I can't say there was any particular extra poignancy to the views we were taking in because we were going home, just a joyful feeling of being alive and moving our bodies.

It took just over two hours to complete the descent. Two hours of sore toes and aching knees, until all of a sudden we caught a distant view of our motorhome several hundred metres beneath us. It was still there, waiting for us.

As is so often the case, the closer we got the more it hurt. There was a definite impatience in our throbbing feet as we raced down the final few muddy tracks to emerge on Pralognan's high street, passing the shops that we'd happily browsed in search of new, exciting gear to take with us on our next adventure. Yet now that adventure had finished. Just a few more metres and we'd be done.

The final steps to the motorhome were emotional ones. I was glad it was over, yet I was sad in equal measure as I leaned my tired body forward to rest my head against the side of the big white box we're fortunate to call home.

Vital Statistics – Day 15
Start: Refuge de la Leisse
End: Pralognan-le-Vanoise
Distance Hiked: 17 kilometres
Hiking Time: 5 hours
Height Gain: 420 metres
Height Loss: 1490 metres

Made It

Now what do we do? With the windows of our motorhome open to let in the morning chill, we sat staring up at the hills we'd explored feeling somewhat lost. It hadn't been a bad little adventure. Fifteen days, more than 250 kilometres of hiking and 14 kilometres of ascent. Added to our Matterhorn tour, that bought us up to almost 600 kilometres for the summer, with 40 vertical kilometres. But that's just numbers, and numbers don't tell the full story. They certainly didn't talk about how much my bloody feet hurt.

If I closed my eyes I could still transport myself back to any of the many incredible places we'd stood, slept and smiled over the preceding weeks. It felt good to do so, but I also knew I couldn't cling on to those memories for too long. They'd fade and change and slowly become part of the tapestry I like to imagine is me, which would be true, but again, still not the full story.

The only place the 'full story' had ever existed had been in the moments when we'd stood in those places, when we'd watched the birds circling, when we'd sat to watch the moon rise and when we'd held hands beneath the stars.

Someone once suggested to me that life is like a river. We can choose to look downstream, idolising all of the moments that have passed us by and regretting the opportunities we think we've missed, or we can turn around.

It was time to look upstream, to whatever adventures lay ahead of us. The next one would start in just two days' time.

Epilogue

I dropped Esther off at the bus station at 7 a.m. on a sleepy Sunday morning, which was good because driving a motorhome through the centre of Lyon at any other time would have given me an aneurysm. If I'd known we weren't going to see each other for an entire month I might have said something profound. Instead, I said "get out quick before the traffic lights change."

Ahead of me was three thousand kilometres of driving, family visits in the UK and three ginger dogs waiting to be collected (though they didn't know it yet). Ahead of Esther was a six hour bus ride and two more ginger dogs in the south of France.

Choosing to split up for a week or so had been a practical decision, intended mostly to save some driving miles. That Esther might do a few days of hiking with Bella and Rose for company while I was gone had been a bit of an afterthought.

Initially, I'd been sceptical. "Why struggle?" I'd asked. "Why not just relax and rest? Hiking with two dogs on your own sounds tricky. Besides, aren't you tired?"

Still, after listening to my challenges she said "I'm doing this, I'd like your support", so that's what she got. Together, we'd fished out our old, awkward but less heavy tent and prepared her pack for a possible solo trip. She told me she wouldn't make a decision until she'd got to our friend's house, yet by the time I was knocking on my grandparents' door she was hiking alone through the Pyrenees.

She ended up trekking for another month, bouncing from cabin to cabin, encountering the kindness of strangers on a daily basis and giving Bella and Rose the adventure of their lives. But that's a story only she can tell.

Thank You

Hello wonderful reader and thank you for making it all the way to the end of *Walking Through Paradise*, the third and currently final book in the Alpine Thru-Hiking series.

I hope that you enjoyed joining us on our meandering adventure. I also hope you can take something from this book away with you. A smile, an idea, or maybe even the seed of your own future journey. Then again, sometimes the best adventures are those that sneak up on us while we're not looking.

It would be wonderful if you'd take a few seconds to leave a review on Amazon. Your review is very important and need only take a matter of seconds.

And, if you haven't already, do take a moment to look at the first two books in this series where we adventure around Mont Blanc and the Matterhorn. More details are given at the end of this book.

Thank you.

Acknowledgements

Arthur and Merlin. Wallace and Gromit. Mr Bean and his Teddy. A team in sync has the power to be greater than the sum of their parts, and that is certainly the case with my own teammate on life's grand adventure.

Whether she's dragging me over blizzard-ridden passes, driving me around Europe in a living room on wheels, or claiming to have found another treehouse we can sleep in, Esther is the driving force behind most of the excitement in our life. I keep telling her I only want a cup of tea.

As with all of my books, this adventure and the words that have followed from it have been a joint project from start to finish.

Thank you, I love you.

Dan Colegate - 2020

www.estheranddan.com

www.instagram.com/estheranddan

www.facebook.com/estheranddan

Photos

1 – Through a garden of cairns beneath the Col de Chavière (2796 metres)

2 – One of many noisy marmots on our way to Refuge de la Femma

3 – Another day, another boulder field. Climbing towards Colle dei Becchi (2990 metres)

4 – Crossing into Italy via the Col de la Lose (2957 metres)

5 – "Baby it's cold outside" – Hiding in Bivacco Giraudo as the weather slowly improves and the snow starts to melt (2630 metres)

6 – A walk on the wild side. Trekking around the Gran Paradiso and not
a soul in sight on the Bocchetta del Ges (2692 metres).

7 – Nearly there. The snow is almost gone a few hundred metres from
the end of the Glacier di Ciardoney (2800 metres)

8 – Looking south from the Col di Bardoney (2833 metres).

9 – Batman and Robin style towards the Colle Gran Neyron (3295 metres).

10 – Moonrise over Bivacco Revelli, our idyllic country-cottage style home for a night (2610 metres).

11 – High above the Vallon de la Leisse (2700 metres)

12 – Our 'treehouse' just outside of Val d'Isere.

These are just a few images from many thousands. For more photos from our adventures, visit our website at **www.estheranddan.com** or our Instagram page **www.instagram.com/estheranddan**

Also By The Author

What Adventures Shall We Have Today?
Travelling From More To Less In Search Of A Simpler Life

You've read one small part of our adventures, now read about the rest! The perfect book for anyone who has ever felt there could be more to life.

Six years ago Dan and Esther were counting down the days until their wedding and the honeymoon of their dreams. Then Dan almost died. Told to say goodbye to each other "just in case" in the early hours of a sleeting January morning, that was the moment when their lives would change forever. Three months later they drove away from their home, their jobs and everything they'd ever known in a second-hand motorhome. Friends and family asked "What do you want to see? Where do you want to go?". All they could say in response was "it's a feeling we're searching for."

At first they planned to travel for a year but as their outlook on life evolved, their priorities changed and they started to get glimpses of 'that feeling', their escape quickly morphed into a lifestyle all of its own.

This is the story of their travels for the past six years. With no plan and no purpose beyond living in the moment, their meandering adventures have taken them over mountains, under the sea, inside of pyramids and across the skies. They've crashed a hot air balloon by the Nile, adopted a dog who surprised them by being pregnant and even became organic farmers for a while, among other things. More than anything, however, they've found themselves confronting their own insecurities and limiting beliefs about how life is supposed to be lived.

This is more than a story of two people drifting around Europe, it's about looking at the world through fresh eyes, reassessing what's truly important and embracing the inevitable challenges that life throws up.

Visit **www.estheranddan.com** or Amazon to find out more.

Turn Left At Mont Blanc: Hiking The TMB

One Couple's Inspirational, Funny & Brutally Honest Account Of Their Adventure Around Europe's Highest Mountain

A hiking story that makes you want to dust off your boots and head straight to the nearest mountains.

The first book in the Alpine Thru-Hiking series. Three years before the adventures in this book, back when Dan and Esther were even less experienced mountain walkers, they flew to Geneva with a bag full of gear, an unopened guidebook and a vague idea that they'd start by walking south.

What happened next was a life-changing adventure.

From one stunning viewpoint to another, from valley to col, from acts of random kindness to moments of unbelievable fortune, this was an adventure that pushed them to the limits of their bodies, their relationship and forced them to face up to some of their deepest fears.

And they got to spend a night in a real teepee!

Written in a light-hearted but direct manner, this is a funny, inspiring and brutally honest account of what it was like to head into the mountains unprepared, under-planned and over-geared and come out on the other side with a whole new outlook on life.

Visit **www.estheranddan.com** or Amazon to find out more.

One Couple's Incredible Adventure

TURN LEFT at MONT BLANC

DAN COLEGATE

Just Around The Matterhorn

Lose yourself in the heart of the Alps, in the shadow of Europe's most iconic mountain.

The second book in the Alpine Thru-Hiking series. Just days before setting off into the Vanoise National Park, Dan and Esther find themselves dog-free and eager to set out into the wilderness. They decide to try the Tour of the Matterhorn, but with no fixed itinerary or timeframe, they find themselves taking a somewhat different route as they hike and camp higher than they've ever been before.

Having started out determined to "take it easy", they instead find themselves pushing their boundaries across glaciers, precipitous ridges and vertical laddered cliffs while also battling illness and at times being hardly able to eat.

Taking in the entire Tour of the Matterhorn and Tour of Monte Rosa (the second highest mountain in the Alps), the remainder of the Chamonix-to-Zermatt Haute Route and a little of the Tour des Combins, their four week odyssey becomes a deep exploration of the finest scenery the Alps has to offer. With almost 25 vertical kilometres of ascent over 320 kilometres of hiking, surrounded by dozens of famous 4000 metre summits, monumental glaciers and remote mountain valleys, it's an adventure not to be missed.

Visit **www.estheranddan.com** or Amazon to find out more.

Printed by Amazon Italia Logistica S.r.l.
Torrazza Piemonte (TO), Italy